The LIVING WORD

Also by Harold Klemp

Animals Are Soul Too!

The Art of Spiritual Dreaming

Ask the Master, Books 1 and 2

Autobiography of a Modern Prophet

Child in the Wilderness

A Cosmic Sea of Words: The ECKANKAR Lexicon

ECK Masters and You: An Illustrated Guide

ECK Wisdom Temples, Spiritual Cities, & Guides: A Brief History

Is Life a Random Walk?

The Living Word, Books 1 and 2

A Modern Prophet Answers Your Key Questions about Life

Past Lives, Dreams, and Soul Travel

Soul Travelers of the Far Country

The Spiritual Exercises of ECK

The Spiritual Laws of Life

The Temple of ECK

Those Wonderful ECK Masters

The Wind of Change

Wisdom of the Heart, Books 1 and 2

Your Road Map to the ECK Teachings: ECKANKAR Study Guide

Youth Ask a Modern Prophet about Life, Love, and God

The Mahanta Transcripts Series

Journey of Soul, Book 1

How to Find God, Book 2

The Secret Teachings, Book 3

The Golden Heart, Book 4

Cloak of Consciousness, Book 5

Unlocking the Puzzle Box, Book 6

The Eternal Dreamer, Book 7

The Dream Master, Book 8

We Come as Eagles, Book 9

The Drumbeat of Time, Book 10

What Is Spiritual Freedom? Book 11

How the Inner Master Works, Book 12

The Slow Burning Love of God, Book 13

The Secret of Love, Book 14

Our Spiritual Wake-Up Calls, Book 15

How to Survive Spiritually in Our Times, Book 16

The Immortality of Soul Series

The Awakened Heart

The Language of Soul

Love—The Keystone of Life

Touching the Face of God

Truth Has No Secrets

Spiritual Wisdom Series

Spiritual Wisdom on Conquering Fear

Spiritual Wisdom on Health and Healing

Spiritual Wisdom on Relationships

Stories to Help You See God in Your Life

The Book of ECK Parables, Volumes 1, 2, and 3

Stories to Help You See God in Your Life, ECK Parables, Book 4

MAHANTA

This book has been authored by and published under the supervision of the Mahanta, the Living ECK Master, Sri Harold Klemp. It is the Word of ECK.

The LIVING WORD

BOOK 3

HAROLD KLEMP

ECKANKAR
Minneapolis
www.Eckankar.org

The Living Word, Book 3

Copyright © 2007 ECKANKAR

Printed in USA

Library of Congress Control Number: 89-086022
ISBN: 978-1-57043-229-3

Compiled by Mary Carroll Moore
Edited by Patrick Carroll, Joan Klemp, and Anthony Moore
Text illustrations by Valerie W. Mortensen
Author photo by Robert Huntley

♾ This paper meets the requirements of ANSI/NISO Z39.48-1992 (Permanence of Paper).

CONTENTS

FOREWORD

*T*he teachings of ECK define the nature of Soul. You are Soul, a particle of God sent into the worlds (including earth) to gain spiritual experience.

The goal in ECK is spiritual freedom in this lifetime, after which you become a Co-worker with God, both here and in the next world. Karma and reincarnation are primary beliefs.

Key to the ECK teachings is the Mahanta, the Living ECK Master. He has the special ability to act as both the Inner and Outer Master for ECK students. The prophet of Eckankar, he is given respect but is not worshiped. He teaches the sacred name of God, HU. When sung just a few minutes each day, HU will lift you spiritually into the Light and Sound of God—the ECK (Holy Spirit). This easy spiritual exercise and others will purify you. You are then able to accept the full love of God in this lifetime.

Sri Harold Klemp is the Mahanta, the Living ECK Master today. Author of many books, discourses, and articles, he teaches the ins and outs of the spiritual life. His teachings lift people and help them recognize and understand their own experiences in the Light and Sound of God. Many of his talks are available to you on audio and video recordings.

The Living Word, Book 3, is a collection of articles he wrote from 1996 to 2005. Ranging from basic to more esoteric ECK teachings, they show how to take knowledge and experience of the Light and Sound of God into your everyday life.

To find out more about Harold Klemp and Eckankar, please turn to page 321 in the back of this book.

Set your sights high. Set them very high. Why not set your sights on God?

CHAPTER ONE

Who Are You as Soul?

1
Your State of Consciousness Is Your State of Acceptance

*L*et's give this letter a name and call it "your state of consciousness is your state of acceptance." There may be some confusion about the phrase *state of consciousness*. What exactly does it mean?

In brief, an individual's state of consciousness simply means his ability to accept change in his life. It includes new thoughts and new feelings, and the new behavior and actions that will naturally come as a result.

A state of consciousness is also flexible in that it swells (expands) and shrinks (contracts). Some events in our lives make us full of joy and goodwill, another way of saying an expansion of consciousness. Other events leave us suspicious or hostile or gloomy—a contraction. There are temporary changes in one's state of consciousness as well as more long-lasting ones, the sum of all the lesser changes.

So your state of consciousness is a living thing. After all, it is a reflection of you—Soul—and is a

Your state of consciousness is a reflection of you—Soul.

3

product of each and every experience you've ever had. Ever.

Different experiences make for the difference in people.

Different experiences make for the difference in people.

The human race as a whole also has a state of consciousness, or level of acceptance. This ability does shift with the passage of time. Sometimes it moves ahead spiritually. At other times, there is a shift to a lower state.

For example, mankind had made some nice gains in the expansion of its world by the first millennium AD. Let's overlook its never-ending lust for war and conquest, which will endure as long as human passions go unchecked. People had learned to make a record in writing of their exploits so future generations might profit by it if they so chose. A written language made it possible to review past mistakes and go on from there. A few, advanced in consciousness, had set down codes of conduct for society: like the sayings of Confucius, the ten commandments of Moses, the thoughts of Socrates and Plato, to name a few.

Those were signs of mankind's progress in its state of consciousness.

Yet there were the dark times too. The most glaring example is perhaps the Dark Ages in Europe, usually fixed from the fifth through the tenth century. Some historians claim the only reason to call it a "dark" period is because so little written history survives from then. That is exactly the point. Why is there so little in writing? There was a falling back in consciousness as the Christian Church also became a political force in Europe and stifled new information.

But even as late as the seventeenth century,

Galileo still felt the sting of the Inquisition, which censored his observation—made with his new invention, the telescope—that not all heavenly bodies revolved around the earth. His support of the Copernican heliocentric system shook the foundations of the church. It called the theory a heresy.

The Dark Ages reflect a retreat in the state of consciousness.

Every person has a unique state of consciousness, even as does every community, town, city, state, region, country, or continent. The same holds for races, religions, political groups, and every other association that comes to mind. For example, who would say there's no difference in the teachings of Islam and Buddhism? The unique doctrines of each are merely an expression of two different states of consciousness, or the acceptance of certain universal ideas that appeal more to one group than the other.

So a state of consciousness is the level of acceptance that one has to changes in conditions.

For some of a certain temperament, blind faith in salvation is a comfort. It gives them courage. They are relieved by the idea that a more advanced spiritual person will take care of all the details when this life comes to an end and will assure them a happy, joyful existence in the hereafter. And that's OK.

People of another state of consciousness may have a more hands-on approach to the issue of death, which punctuates human life for many with a question mark. Their state of consciousness says, "It's up to each of us to find our own salvation."

Is it any wonder that so much of our history is penned in blood? No human state of consciousness is of a shining purity. Each has its stains. These stains are from the five passions of lust, greed,

Every person has a unique state of consciousness, even as does every community, town, city, state, region, country, or continent.

anger, vanity, and an undue attachment to material things. But their state of consciousness does determine how darkly these stains color the behavior of people toward each other.

People relate to a given set of conditions in keeping with their capacity to accept change, as said earlier. But how does this ability come about?

Human joy and suffering in everyday life are always on hand, to build and shape our outlook on the events that face us without end. Experience leads us to love and compassion. A child may carry into adulthood the memory of a grandmother, on one side of the family, who was gentle, good, and kind. Yet its memory of the other grandmother may be quite the opposite. The second grandmother, about the same age as the first, leaves behind a memory of telling bawdy jokes, embarrassing the clergyman, and taking life with a wink.

It's all about two states of consciousness.

Your own state of consciousness is nothing more than the amount of love you can accept from God.

How open, loving, and forgiving are we? The ECK Master Rebazar Tarzs says, "Purity calls for the highest within man. You cannot slander nor can you see the evil in others" (*Stranger by the River*, "Purity").

Ah, but we should also note what he adds: "Dwell upon the good within thy neighbor and thus you will exalt the good in him, and bring out the good in thyself." *That is a spiritual exercise.*

Now you should have a better idea about your own state of consciousness, for it is nothing more than the amount of love you can accept from God.

And give love as it has been given to you.

2
The Wonder of You

Who could be more wonderful than you? You have, oh, so many blessings. All you need to do is recognize them.

Can you? Will you? Do you?

Look around. You live in a garden. Someone loved you so much that here you are, in a garden. There is spiritual food all around, there to feed and nourish. All you need to do is get it.

You are one of the special people. Somehow you've become awake and opened your eyes. Now awake, you know you are special. You know you live in a very special garden, a garden of love. Someone loved you so much that you are here, and awake. What a blessing to know you are blessed.

So how'd you come to be? How'd you get here? Why? And where to next?

Questions in the midst of plenty. Thinking, thinking. Why, why? And, why, why?

All this and more is you, a so-wonderful you.

Handmade in heaven.

Cared for on earth.

And all you have to do is accept it, and you will recognize the wonder of you too.

You are one of the special people. You've become awake and opened your eyes.

Set your sights high. Set them very high. Why not set your sights on God? Sugmad (God) loves you and has from Its creation of you. You're handmade in heaven, by the Maker of life, love, freedom, and happiness too. Be happy, be you, just BE!

Put away your fear. Put away your doubt. And remember to put away your worry.

You are Soul. Special. One of a kind. So love yourself, love God, and love others. That's what your stay in this place is to help you learn. So look around and say thank you for all the blessings. Be grateful. Make sure this is a fruitful life. After all, why be here if you won't?

Such is the wonder of you. Wake up and sing! Glory in this garden of love, because the holy foods are all around. The best is yet to come.

*   *   *

We've made our world and all that's in it.

Now let's leave creation and being from beyond the stars and return to the world of being that we've created. We've made our world and all that's in it. Slowly and surely we see that it is so.

Our realization of it has a starting point, a place where Soul's awakening begins in earnest.

This launching pad is the Second Initiation. Let's see how Soul may come to it. And what then? Let's also look at two recent ECKists, a First and a Second Initiate. Both their names have been changed.

Lucia is a First Initiate. She's been in Eckankar less than a year to date.

Before one can begin the big spiritual awakening, he must find the teachings of ECK. A friend introduced her to them when she was at a university in 1992. This was in the British West Indies. She received an Eckankar brochure and also learned that those wishing to receive truth must be willing to share the modest cost it takes to provide it. This calls for self-responsibility. It came as a shock to Lucia, however. So she did not become a member.

She nevertheless began to do the spiritual exercise of singing HU, our love song to God, given in the brochure. Her experiences with the Light and Sound of God began at once. They continue still.

This had been her situation:

Lucia was a devout Roman Catholic all her life. But her spiritual hunger was growing, unsatisfied by her church. She felt there was more to the "Me" she was. Where, oh where, could she find out about that?

Then, suddenly, there was Eckankar.

Her spiritual hunger had called for something to quiet the insistent longing in her to develop a personal and deep communion with God. This, she felt, would make sense of her existence.

The very night of the day she'd received the brochure she had a dream. Three men greeted her.

"Welcome to ECK," they said.

It was a realistic dream, but she was cautious. "How am I to know this is real?" she asked. Her house was nearby.

In response, a large wave of water rushed through it, but disturbing nothing and hurting no one. Her house, though, was left clean and spotless. And with the housecleaning came a marvelous feeling of warmth and being cared for. It stayed with her a very long time.

Yet she didn't commit to Eckankar. It'd be three years until she did. In the meantime, she learned about karma and how it worked. Also about not intruding into the thoughts and deeds of others. Yet

Lucia felt there was more to the "Me" she was. Where, oh where, could she find out about that?

it wasn't enough. Her spiritual hunger grew.

Suddenly, in 1995, she decided to return to her hometown, which had an ECK center. She became a true Hound of Heaven. She'd found the trail, the scent of truth was strong, and she'd follow it to the very end. So Lucia read every ECK book that came her way. She went to every HU Chant or ECK seminar.

Sound and Light experiences were with her from the very beginning, like the yellow light. Sounds too, like the chiming of bells. And many, many meetings with the Mahanta, the Inner Master.

Now Lucia is more content and loves herself and others more. She's compelled to do loving things for others.

*   *   *

Jim's a new Second Initiate. Before and after he received the initiation, his life seemed to fall apart. Old things broke and needed replacing.

So begins Soul's awakening to the wonder of you.

His car was one of them. One day, he left it by the roadside, a steaming, smoking piece of junk. He'd need a new used car. But inspection showed all of them unfit to make a reliable commute from country to city. His wife said to check out a new/used car dealer she'd found and look for a used one there.

So he went. It was a large dealership, with several entrances. The Mahanta guided him to an "off-lot lot," where cars were sold that the dealer felt had better prospects there. Jim found his car.

Jim realized that his old car was him before the Second Initiation, the new one is him now. The old one had gone as far as it could. The new one can take him where he needs to go. He's learning.

And so begins Soul's awakening to the wonder of you.

3
How to Find
Freedom from Yourself

What do you suppose makes people unhappy? A survey would probably list a hundred reasons, both real and imagined.

Now how many of those people do you think would like to hear the true reason for their unhappiness? Just a guess—very few.

The choices you've made in the past are the direct cause of all your unhappiness today.

If this answer doesn't suit you, don't read another word. You have better things to do. But maybe you're one of the few people who doesn't absolutely reject the above explanation for your unhappiness. Then keep reading. Perhaps you'll see *how* and *why* individuals make bad choices.

Most important, you may learn how to stop making them.

Let's start with a few examples of how poor decisions in past lives contributed to one person's lack of freedom and unhappiness in this lifetime.

We'll call her Shelley to insure her privacy. Shelley knows about karma. It's a repayment, or balancing of books, for our past misdeeds, but also

11

for acts of generosity. Old missteps cause us pain today. On the other hand, past generosity to others is the reason for any happiness that offsets the pain. The balance between them makes life more bearable.

Old missteps cause us pain today.

Shelley does the Spiritual Exercises of ECK every day. So the Mahanta, the Inner Master, showed her three earlier lives to provide an insight into her grapplings with misplaced worth and identity in relation to others.

In short, these three past lives left her feeling worth less than other people. That attitude has caused her a lot of agony in this lifetime.

Here follows a brief summary of these earlier lives.

• *Past Life Number 1*

She calls the first past life the "Vanity Queen" lifetime.

Shelley was a queen then, a woman of power, influence, and beauty in a long-ago time and place. She gave her attendants shabby treatment—as some people in power do—while her attendants lavished care upon her. Her slightest wish was their command.

Her designers lived to dress her, a beautiful and striking woman. *God must have a reason for giving me this beauty*, she thought.

On top of that, God had also given her much intelligence in the popular sense. A good sense of intuition rounded out her arsenal. It made her believe she could outthink people most of the time, and she used all these inner talents to protect her ego. A sad abuse of power.

In looking back at that lifetime, Shelley realized that all mistakes then, subtle and glaring, were embedded in her own choices.

A spirit of charity would have been easy. God had given her many advantages, and there were countless goods at her disposal to share with others. But she was stingy when it came to acts of generosity and charity. They had to be her idea. She refused to give help when others needed or expected it on the grounds that it would sacrifice her freedom of choice.

Shelley was the darling of the times, but she was like a spider in the bed.

The Mahanta let her see that her choices were those of immaturity and selfishness over love. Shelley had hardly made wise choices.

In this lifetime, she realizes the great debt she owes her dear parents, once helpless subjects of her abuse and neglect. The Mahanta, the Inner Master, would reveal to her the consequences of such immaturity and wretched behavior during two later lifetimes.

The Law of Karma then came into play. Shelley lost the opportunity to choose, even to the point of losing the right of her own opinions.

Shelley was the darling of the times, but she was like a spider in the bed.

- ● *Past Life Number 2*

Next, the Mahanta let her revisit a lifetime in which she was the mistress of a low-level political appointee. He was only a remote member of a royal family that was in power hundreds of years ago. A nobody.

Yet he provided her well with material goods. There were plenty of fine clothes and an abundance of food.

In return, he got a beautiful consort. She had an ageless, childlike face with big eyes, full lips and cheeks, and shiny golden brown hair that rippled like a river of light. Her owner prized her above all other women, so she never faced the threat of replacement.

But people around her regarded her as one might luncheon meat. They never let her forget their scorn.

It left her with feelings of low worth—mentally, emotionally, and spiritually—right into the present lifetime.

That sheltered life was one in which she lacked power of any sort. From birth she was unequal. She accepted her lot with loneliness and vacancy. Unable to even control her own beauty, she was only a plaything for her owner.

• *Past Life Number 3*

The Mahanta then opened her vision to the next lifetime.

The Mahanta then opened her vision to the next lifetime. It was another echo of that first life, even as the second had been. Again, with some power returned to her by the Lords of Karma, she ended up making more poor choices.

Reincarnated as a male, she joined the church around the time of the Inquisition. She rose quickly in the hierarchy due to her obedience to church disciplines and an absolute commitment to the letter of the law. Her lack of imagination was evident, but it was amply rewarded by her strict obedience to church law. Soon, she was a full participant in the Inquisition.

She loved to torture victims. Their cries could not touch her heart, because she had few feelings of her own. Shelley was perfect for the job. Only the church had value. Unmoved by human suffering, she was an ideal machine for the evils of the time.

So in this lifetime, Shelley's been sickened by man's inhumanity to man—the least of her troubles from her cruelty to others then.

Most of those past-life debts are paid up, thanks to all the help from the Mahanta, the Living ECK Master and the Spiritual Exercises of ECK. Her obligations to her parents, among others, are nearly all in balance now. These lessons from the past have taken her from spiritual immaturity to divine love.

The fast lane to freedom can be yours, too, in Eckankar.

4
The Spiritually Great

A distinguishing mark of people who achieve stature in any field is faith. They believe in a goal, idea, or principle. And they hold to their dream beyond every defeat.

So also the spiritually great. Earth is a preparatory school for spiritual greatness, with all its tests, failures, and successes. But each class is of one, a single person. No group—whether of family, politics, religion, or philosophy—can assure the well-rounded education of any Soul.

For that very reason life offers us variety. Within certain boundaries, we may pick and choose as we please.

Early in an individual's development into a well-rounded spiritual being, the Kal (negative power) has an easy time of it, passing off to him the idea of "something for nothing." It sells. Immature Souls take the bait every time. Notice the popularity of lotteries, gambling, or lawsuits to seize property not theirs by right. (No, man's law is not the final determinant of God's law.)

Expectations.

It's a key word behind the seduction of people to put faith in the security of material goods. Like,

Earth is a preparatory school for spiritual greatness, with all its tests, failures, and successes.

say, the stock (or share) market. A run-up in that quarter finances homes, cars, vacations, electronic toys, gadgets for home and office, and much waste.

Yet material goods do have a rightful place. Money does give one more freedom in some respects than does a lack of it. A retirement plan makes good sense in many societies.

Even a professional gambler can earn a rightful living at the gaming tables, but it's likely he worked hard to develop his profession. He trained and thus gains. And there are even honorable brokers, those who help people manage their funds through proven methods of investment. Yet clients must pay for those services.

Life gives all people a lot of wiggle room to follow a chosen path of spiritual development.

Life gives all people a lot of wiggle room to follow a chosen path of spiritual development. In that sense, there's no right or wrong.

Unless, unless one ventures to steal the rights or property of another by stealth or force. Life hands out a judgment for that. Its name is karma. Yet remember, karma encompasses the good returns too. And within the all-reaching grasp of the Law of Karma is the play of every action and reaction in these lower worlds of matter, energy, space, and time.

Expectations.

Dr. Raj Persaud at Maudsley Hospital in London gave an explanation of the seductive force of expectations upon people. In a letter to the editor of *The Economist*, he said:

"[A]n old finding from psychological research is pertinent; it seems the more you give people, the greater their subsequent expectations of life. Yet it is a widening gap between your expectations and what you actually have which predicts unhappiness."

Dr. Persaud has a clear insight into the link between expectations and unhappiness.

He goes on to observe how the British National Lottery offers big winners the chance to get counseling, so they may stay content in spite of new wealth. No doubt, there is a need for it. What irony! The lack of spiritual wealth obtained by some big winners shows that money is not the gilded road to happiness.

When big lottery winners leave earth, the material riches stay behind, of course, but the spiritual largess carries with them to the other worlds. In a sense, they do take it with them.

Maybe that's the reason that some Souls are big lottery winners.

The experience of living teaches them about the falsity of prosperity as the path to the secret kingdom. The small of mind and heart, the greedy, the miserly, the foolish—all will see the consequences brought on by the little self. And no earthly reward can offer lasting peace.

Who knows, in a later lifetime on earth a former lottery winner may brush aside the sweet, seductive whispers of Kal, who will need to unbox a whole new package of enticements.

The old ones have fulfilled their purpose. That Soul is a little wiser about spiritual values than in the previous incarnation.

A spiritual giant in the making.

What, then, will quiet the heart if not gold, silver, fame, or some other material gain?

Henry David Thoreau, the nineteenth-century American writer, put his finger on the effect upon people who search for the elusive holy grail of contentment but never find it. "The mass of men

What, then, will quiet the heart if not gold, silver, fame, or some other material gain?

lead lives of quiet desperation and go to the grave with the song still in them."

That song is the joy that comes of finding the Light and Sound of God. Together, they are the Melody of Life.

The true Word of God.

*   *   *

So we do not begrudge others the fruit of material success. But we give joy to the Children of Light and Sound for the happy discovery of the ECK teachings. They remain the font of all riches of a lasting kind. So with George Washington, first U.S. president, we say: "Show not yourself glad at the misfortune of another, though he were your enemy."

The ECK teachings remain the font of all riches of a lasting kind.

The teachings of ECK center upon the principle "Soul exists because of God's love for It." Eckankar is therefore the religion of love—divine love. It touches all things. We love others to such an extent that we avoid offering them false expectations about material success and its dreamed-of happiness. We will tell no one to join ECK to gain health or wealth.

But wisdom? Oh, yes.

A Higher Initiate tells of someone who had a question about *vairag*, the mental detachment from worldly desires and things. "Why is it called the Order of the Vairagi and not the Order of Love?" he asked.

The Mahanta had earlier in the month given the H.I. a glimpse of the reason. In a dream, she stood at the top of a windy mountain with the Master. He surrounded her with a column of space. This giving of space created a greater intensity of love, she says, than she'd ever felt.

It is for that very reason the mystic Adepts

carry the spiritual name of the Order of the Vairagi rather than perhaps the expected Order of Love.

Direct experience lent this H.I. a priceless gem of wisdom.

Spiritual greatness, like life, is the journey. It's not the destination. While there are markers along the way, they are but markers. You are the journey itself. The spiritual teachings of ECK teach the long view. Why sell out your chance at true greatness for the off-key promise of happiness through the gathering of material goods? They are like phantoms that last but a night.

My mission is to help you become one of the spiritually great. So let's keep at it.

My mission is to help you become one of the spiritually great.

5
How to Find Spiritual Freedom in This Lifetime

A belief drummed into me as a boy about life after death had little appeal. It was that at death Soul "sleeps" until the final day of judgment, a time of unconsciousness.

A belief drummed into me as a boy about life after death had little appeal.

How My Search Began

I grew up on a farm. Family life revolved around raising and caring for cattle as a livelihood, planting the crops to feed them and us, and just as important, going to our country church for services. Church was a social center. Of course, we all came to worship God, but most of us found the visit with neighbors later outside just as fulfilling.

Nearly everyone in church was related. It's natural, then, that everyone knew everyone else very well. A church service was a weekly reunion of relatives.

During those years, Grandpa and Grandma often lived with one of their children on the family farm. The grandparents were wise and beloved elders, for the most part. They helped care for the grandchildren, did light chores, and gave instruction to their

23

grown children. In time, of course, one by one, the old ones would pass on.

The day of the funeral was generally like a Sunday in that farmers only did the regular morning and evening chores. It was a sad day of worship.

But children were on hand during the time before a grandparent's passing. The process of dying had not yet become sanitized as it often is today, when the sick and elderly go to age and die away from home. It all happened before our eyes. We came to grips with death on many occasions. Death meant the loss of someone near and dear, not the mysterious departure of someone seen only a few times a year on a festive vacation.

Even more than that, a farm child watched his parents and neighbors get ready for the funeral. He heard them on the phone. They'd call each other to express sorrow, offer consolation, and perhaps, give a gentle commentary about the good deeds in the departed one's life.

The final good-byes were said at church. Whole families, from baby to the most feeble elder, would come to the funeral service if health and weather allowed.

It was at funerals that doubts began to grow in my mind about the "sleep" state of Soul.

Our congregation first listened to the pastor give the funeral blessings. Then, the entire assembly filed out to the cemetery alongside the church where the coffin disappeared into a dark hole, whose piles of dirt were spruced up with green ground cloths. We boys stayed to watch the assigned farmers close the grave. Last, into the church basement for a meal of fellowship.

The Beginning of Doubt

It was at funerals that doubts began to grow in my mind about the "sleep" state of Soul. Everyone just assumed that the deceased's body and Soul were pretty much one and the same.

True, the physical body would soon decay and be eaten by worms, but on the Last Day a more glorious body would rise from the grave.

What kid wouldn't give his eyeteeth to be at the cemetery on that great day to watch the spectacle of a lifetime—the opening of graves and all these people helping each other out of the ground? Wouldn't that be a splendid show? (Better than a county fair!) Yet for all the promise of excitement, a dark cloud hovered over this one-of-a-kind picture. What were the odds this spectacular event would come in my lifetime? A million to one. That left at least this farm boy with a most unhappy prospect. Would I be another of the millions—billions—of unlucky Souls trapped in a dark hole for maybe a thousand years?

And what if I failed to awaken from the sleep of death?

Over time, funerals got more and more of my attention. You could say I was looking for something better. Unknowingly, I'd become a seeker.

A Seeker Is Born

The seeker!

Indeed, there was an awakening from sleep as I passed from boy to young man. It came slowly, at the most unexpected times.

What was that mysterious humming sound at night when I was two and three? My brother, two years older, and I still slept in our parents' bedroom, so my tiny voice pierced the darkness.

"What is that humming?"

But neither Mother nor Dad could hear it. "It's the electric wires outside," they said. "Now go to

You could say I was looking for something better. Unknowingly, I'd become a seeker.

sleep." Dad's alarm rang at four o'clock, to wake him for morning chores. He had no time for such non-sense. Yet as the years passed, my thoughts at night often alighted softly upon those early childhood memories of the mysterious humming sound. Where had it gone? The electric wires still ran outside my open window, but that soothing, almost musical, sound had disappeared over the years.

Some Answers

Later, in Eckankar, I found this humming to be one of the many sounds of God. It was the movement of God's Voice—the Holy Spirit, or ECK—vibrating the ethers of time and space.

To hear one of these sacred sounds is a great joy and blessing.

Anyway, a lot of water passed under the bridge of my life before that revelation came to me. There were other awakenings too. Little ones, in looking back. Yet they were all I could accept at each level of unfoldment. These awakenings included visions, dreams of the future, Soul Travel, and other wonders that left me in awe of the once-hidden mysteries of the Eternal One, God.

They were all directed at one goal: my spiritual freedom in this very lifetime. Here and now. There was no need to enter into a "death sleep" that could last for centuries. Maybe forever. What if my childhood religion had it wrong? Then the risk was all mine.

You are at that point in life, too, where some Voice of God has gently shaken your shoulder to awaken you from a deep spiritual slumber.

You are at that point in life, too, where some Voice of God has gently shaken your shoulder to awaken you from a deep spiritual slumber. Read on to discover more about the most direct road to spiritual freedom—here and now.

Spiritual Exercise: Two-part Door of Soul

The door of Soul opens inward. No amount of pushing on the wrong side will open it.

Twenty minutes to half an hour is the limit to spend on a spiritual exercise during a session unless an experience has begun. Then, of course, see it through to the end.

To set up an experience with the Light and Sound of God or the Inner Master, use this two-part technique:

1. In contemplation sometime during the day, count backward slowly from ten to one. Then try to see yourself standing beside your human self, which is at rest. Keep this part to half an hour or less.

2. The second part of this technique comes at night when you are preparing for sleep. Speak to the Dream Master, the Mahanta. Say to him, "I give you permission to lead me into the Far Country, to the right places and people."

Now go to sleep. Give no further thought to this technique. Your permission to the Mahanta unlocks the unconscious mind and gives the human mind a chance to retain a memory of your dream travels come morning.

That's all there is to this two-part dream exercise.

Be sure a dream notebook is within easy reach. Keep notes. Remember that in the spiritual field, there is no need to push things. With ECK in your life, the gifts of Spirit, like love and wisdom, will now start coming to your attention.

All spiritual good comes with the Spiritual Exercises of ECK.

To set up an experience with the Light and Sound of God or the Inner Master, use this two-part technique.

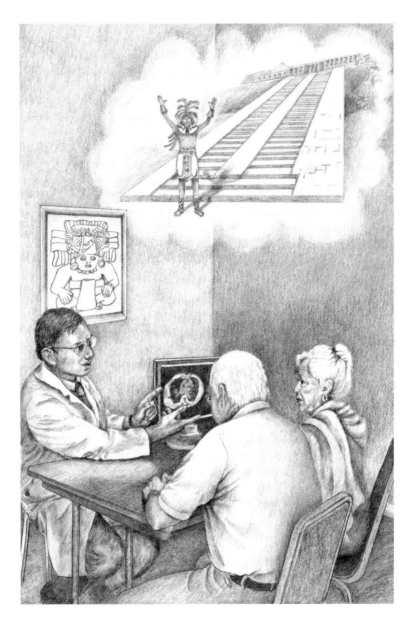

The priest in those ancient days was now their doctor.
His field of service today was to heal hearts.

CHAPTER TWO

Lessons from the Past

6
Past, Present, and Future Lives

There once was a handsome Trojan named Tithonus. Lucky was he to have the love of Eos, goddess of the dawn.

Tithonus prayed to Eos to grant him immortality. But he'd neglected to ask for youth. So in time, like any mortal, Tithonus became aged in body and infirm.

He now offered up a new prayer. Would Eos let him die?

This boon she could not grant, but she could change him into a new physical form. And so, Tithonus became a grasshopper.

*   *   *

Of course, each Soul is eternal—like Tithonus. Unlike him, however, the True Self has no fear of the hand of aging, infirmity, or forgetfulness. It is whole, beyond time. Yet the human bodies It wears during Its many rebirths do see the afflictions that come with the passing of years.

A human shell is like an oak leaf. It buds in spring, enjoys its beauty, vibrancy, and strength in

The True Self has no fear of the hand of aging, infirmity, or forgetfulness. It is whole, beyond time.

31

summer, then turns dry after the chill winds of autumn. In winter, it falls.

But then, spring.

A new bud shoots forth, and a new cycle of life begins.

Soul takes on a new body in like manner. In our human incarnations we are like an oak leaf: a leaf, but not the same oak leaf. In fact, Soul, the immortal, is rather like Tithonus the grasshopper. On each return, we hop from one set of circumstances to a somewhat different set.

And yet, the grasshopper's memory is short. He's aware of one jump at a time. But barely that.

The past is a fascinating study. Even more so is learning of a present condition that saw birth in a past life.

A Grasshopper Remembers the Past

The past is a fascinating study. Even more so is learning of a present condition that saw birth in a past life.

To celebrate their wedding anniversary, a couple took a cruise. A port of call was Mexico. The couple went to see the Mayan ruins at Tulum, took many pictures, and also bathed in the turquoise waters nearby. The cruise was a happy, memorable event.

But it proved to be more than a physical journey.

Soon after their return home, both the woman's husband and her father became ill with the same problem, congestive heart failure. They were taken to the same hospital, the same floor, and shared the same doctor. An interesting quirk of timing and location.

On top of that, the wife, four months before the cruise, had been brought to that very hospital and saw the same doctor, because she too had a heart problem. A small world indeed.

The woman who wrote this account to me is a

member of Eckankar. She reports that it was obviously a spiritual lesson of sorts. But what?

She asked the Mahanta, the Inner Master, for an insight.

Then came a dream. It showed her a past life when she, her husband, even her father, and the doctor were Mayans. On the day of a great festival, crowds of people in bright colors and feathers filled the streets around the temples. The doctor was a high priest. He was at the top of the temple stairs performing human sacrifices. The Mahanta spared her the experience of reliving her family's and her own death.

The dream was clear. The priest who did human sacrifices in those ancient days was now their doctor. His field of service today was to heal hearts, not rip them out.

That's how the Law of Karma deals with misdeeds.

A bright sidelight to the dream is that she had a healing. She no longer needs to take any heart medication.

A dream showed her a past life when she, her husband, even her father, and the doctor were Mayans.

A Grasshopper Spots a Lesson in the Present

Some years ago, a certain employee was in line for a promotion to management. His chances looked good.

The executive in charge of selecting the best of the best was an ECKist, a member of Eckankar. He left the outcome to the ECK, Divine Spirit. Yet he did his part too. He entrusted a number of projects to this candidate to test his people skills. Time proved the candidate's judgment to be unreliable.

Still, the ECKist awaited some confirmation from the ECK.

It came one day when he and his wife went for a drive to run errands. He told her of his observations about the candidate's lack of vision and experience.

At that moment, the ECK sent the couple a waking dream to illustrate the situation in a striking way.

A waking dream is a spiritual insight. It is a show-and-tell example from everyday life that illustrates a principle or point with another event happening at that exact moment.

The ECKist had just mused, "He's a small man inside."

In that same instant, the couple spotted a man no taller than a five-year-old, strolling alongside the road.

"I see what you mean," said his wife, for she was an ECKist too and knew of the miraculous power of the ECK to arrange such a coincidence. No further explanations were needed.

The ECK, Holy Spirit, has an uncanny way of selecting an outer experience to create a waking dream to fit circumstances.

So this employee's talents were turned to good use in other ways rather than a promotion to that managerial opening.

The ECK, Holy Spirit, has an uncanny way of selecting an outer experience to create a waking dream to fit circumstances.

A Grasshopper Wonders about the Future

A grasshopper is curious about things, so he jumps or else flies on the wind. He wants to see afar. Perhaps he wants to know what secrets the future holds.

Most ECKists part company with rebirth on earth after this lifetime. It's one of the benefits of accepting the Mahanta, the Living ECK Master as the steersman of their boat. The bulk of humanity, however, will profit from hundreds of more lives here in their pursuit of spiritual perfection.

What does the distant future hold for them?

For the answer, let's see what the sacred text of *The Shariyat-Ki-Sugmad*, Book One, has to offer on the subject.

"The sixth root race," it says, "is the yellow race, coming on the heels of the gradually fading Aryan race. It is the Mongoloid race of the East, which has its life center in the world of the North, where many do not penetrate. The ECK Master who will come into this world of semidarkness and light will be Regnard. This race is yet to fulfill its destiny on the earth planet. It will meet destruction by fire, earthquakes, and tidal waves."

The future offers exciting, but hard times.

So where does this leave people who return to earth again and again in a new body? They are like Tithonus. The round of births and rebirths will carry them into a tumultuous age. They will hop from life to life, wondering what it's all about.

An ECKist learns it's about spiritual liberation. It's about finding a way out. It's about freedom, joy, and wisdom. It's all about divine love.

Someday, each grasshopper will catch the high wind of ECK and fly to a place of incredible light and beauty.

God's full love awaits them.

An ECKist learns it's about spiritual liberation. It's about finding a way out. It's about freedom, joy, and wisdom. It's all about divine love.

7
Another Look
at *The Shariyat*

At age seven or so, I liked to run off steam before the school day began by racing around our schoolhouse. A crisp autumn morning lent an invigorating air.

Schoolmates, also a few minutes early, stood by the bicycle racks, making small talk until Mr. H. thrust open the schoolhouse door and furiously rang his teacher's bell. By then, I'd run off my steam. Running was a satisfying exercise for a farm boy more comfortable outdoors than lodged behind a desk.

One brisk fall morning, my routine came to an abrupt end. Experience taught me better.

The sprint around the schoolhouse was alone, with my cousin, or a schoolmate. We were like colts, trying out our legs and wind. Usually, though, each of us chose to run alone. On this morning, I took off counterclockwise. Like a race car, I cut the corners short. Dad had taken us to a stock-car race, and now the power of a V-8 engine coursed through me.

Like a race car, I cut the corners short. Racing was living!

Racing was living!

Then I met Vernon. He was two years older. We met on the far corner of the schoolhouse, and the

37

meeting left a strong impression on me. By all accounts, it did on him too.

One second there was an open speedway ahead. The next, a split-second blur of each other, coming head-on.

We bounced off one another, examined the ground on our bellies, then on hands and knees. This experience left a lasting impression. For some days, we were content to forgo that old habit of tearing around the building at full gallop. We were thinking. There was no advantage to that sport without some adjustment.

For my part, the change in habit meant running a wider track around the schoolhouse. Steer wide of blind corners. That lesson has stuck with me to this day.

Of course, the lesson was about change. We do what we do until experience teaches us the wisdom of trying some better course of action.

Life is change. What is life if not about change?

The Shariyat-Ki-Sugmad means the Way of the Eternal. The descriptive title of these holy scriptures of ECK could well be "The Book of Change." It's all about change. The spiritual benefit of *The Shariyat* is that it's a guide to better living.

The spiritual benefit of The Shariyat *is that it's a guide to better living.*

"To improve is to change," Winston Churchill, the British statesman, once observed. "To be perfect is to change often."

Mark Twain, the American writer, said the following, which is an insight into the benefits of change:

"Twenty years from now you will be more disappointed by things you didn't do than by the ones you did do. So throw off the bowlines. Sail away from the safe harbor. Catch the trade winds in your sails. Explore. Dream. Discover."

Change covers a lot of territory.

For example, *The Shariyat* says that "ECKANKAR was revealed to Rama by one of the ancient ECK Masters." The key word here is *revealed*. It means Rama was introduced to something beyond his experience. He was, in fact, lifted out of his body and taken to the city of Agam Des. There, the ancient Master responsible for his revelation showed him the portion of the Shariyat-Ki-Sugmad in safekeeping in that inaccessible world.

It is accessible only by invitation and then only via Soul Travel.

Following his study of the Shariyat, Rama traveled down from the Hindu Kush and brought the teachings of ECK to India.

So you see, the revelation of Rama marked a great change. It changed him from a seeker of truth to its messenger. His desire for truth had thrown wide the gates of heaven. This change, you'll also note, first filled his cup, but then the Law of Divine Love compelled him to share its contents, the water of life, with others who had a thirst for it too.

Today, Rama is known as the first world savior. He taught the people of his times that one could have the experience of God in this very lifetime.

Life is all about change.

Do you recall the stories about the lost continent of Lemuria? It was once a great civilization, home of the third root race. Today, it is considered a fictitious place, even more so than Atlantis. But Lemuria ranged across the mid–Pacific Ocean into China. It developed for centuries. A vast country of low, rolling hills and a soft, pleasant climate, Lemuria seemed invincible to change.

Rama taught the people of his times that one could have the experience of God in this very lifetime.

Then the earth shook, and the tidal waves struck. The people, for the most part peaceful and gentle, found few places of refuge in those awful times of change.

But then, the rumblings ceased. In time, the people overcame their initial fear. They rebuilt their cities. Then, in the blink of eternity's night, earthquakes and tidal waves struck once more, and other parts of Lemuria sank beneath the waters to disappear forever. Little remains to tell of that late, great civilization. Only a few hilltops remained after the upheavals to become the islands of the Pacific.

But, of course, it was hardly the end of civilization. Colonies had been established by then in far places like India and South America. The most important colony, however, was Atlantis.

Atlantis, then, slowly replaced Lemuria as the center of civilization. A new experiment in consciousness occurred on this continent, located in what is today the emptiness of the Atlantic Ocean. Yet, it was a land of black magic. The Atlanteans, the fourth root race, soon destroyed themselves with these dark arts, and Atlantis followed Lemuria into the sea of lost dreams.

The continents may be gone and forgotten by most, yet the lessons remain. Souls who lived many lifetimes in Lemuria came back to try again in many other lives in places and times like Atlantis, Egypt, the Americas, Europe, Asia, India, Africa, and elsewhere.

The lessons go on. People—as individuals and as members of groups like religions, races, political groups, and families—continue to learn about the Law of Love the hard way.

Raw experience is the best teacher of all.

Souls who lived many lifetimes in Lemuria came back to try again in many other lives in places and times like Atlantis, Egypt, the Americas, Europe, Asia, India, Africa, and elsewhere.

So, as a boy, I once learned to temper my racing around the schoolhouse. The lesson was to swing wide of the corners.

The Shariyat-Ki-Sugmad is your guide to a better life. Open it at random each day. Read a paragraph, page, or chapter. Read it with an open heart, and it will open your eyes. That much I promise you.

Also, treat yourself to *The Shariyat* audiobook. Now on audiocassette or CD, it is read at a pace that allows time for reflection.

Look again at *The Shariyat-Ki-Sugmad*. It will soften the changes in your life.

Read The Shariyat-Ki-Sugmad *with an open heart, and it will open your eyes.*

8
Your Key to
the Secret Worlds

A young woman from England stumbled onto the ECK teachings. In a short time she read *How to Find God*, Mahanta Transcripts, Book 2, and *ECKANKAR—Ancient Wisdom for Today*. She felt they were what she had been searching for.

Next she tried some exercises out of the book *The Spiritual Exercises of ECK*. Here's what happened to her:

It was springtime in England then. While walking to her place of work, beams of white light came down on and around her like lightning, but it was silent and gentle. What did this wonderful experience mean? She wondered whether it was to give her some sort of healing, or did it mean she had been lifted in her spiritual consciousness to where God is?

She didn't know.

All she did know, however, was that it was a spiritual experience and that it filled her heart with wonder and love. To her credit, she has patience. Could the Mahanta, the Living ECK Master somehow let her know the meaning of the beams of white light? If not, she would understand and let things be.

Beams of white light came down on and around her like lightning, but it was silent and gentle. What did this wonderful experience mean?

Basically, she had been blessed with the Light of God. Her love for truth had opened her heart to it.

Love was her key to the secret worlds of God.

Dreams are often a golden avenue to these secret worlds. What is a good way to describe dreams in ECK?

Dreams are often a golden avenue to these secret worlds.

Carol, a staff member at the Temple of ECK, gives dream workshops from time to time. One day, while in contemplation, she opened her eyes and saw an hourglass, which struck her as a good way to describe dreams in ECK.

The top of the hourglass, she saw, is the place dreams come from: heaven, a higher consciousness. As the sands (dreams) run down, the dream censor pinches off the flow at the waist of the hourglass. That leaves only censored dreams, or distorted truths, at the bottom of the glass.

Lots of books on dream interpretation in bookstores and libraries try to sort out the distortions with various degrees of success.

But in ECK, Carol says, the dreamer can also go to a higher state of consciousness (top of the hourglass). To the origin of dreams. It's the best place to understand the truths that dreams give to the dreamer. The way to the top of the hourglass, she adds, is simple: through the Spiritual Exercises of ECK and the Dream Master.

They are your key to the secret worlds.

Dreams of past lives can help to explain a person's nature, fears, and relationships. In the following story, Mark and Jennifer (not their real names) learned how a past life together had spilled into their marriage of today. A dream helped them to understand each other better.

Mark has a tendency to be forgetful at home. Jennifer is always there to remind him when he overlooks or forgets something of importance.

As a boy, Mark was often the target of his father's violent rages, in which he was yelled at and cursed when they were together alone. Mark could not understand his father's anger. True, he was an alcoholic. But the reason seemed to go much deeper, likely an old karmic pattern.

About two years ago, Mark had a dream of a past life that began to show him what that old pattern was, the pattern that loaded him down with anger, guilt, shame, and fear. He and Jennifer had been a young couple in that lifetime, with two young children. The period of history was unclear. The family lived in a small, two-story wooden house that burned down one night. The fire consumed all of them.

Then, the window to that past life closed again, leaving a lot of unanswered questions.

At the 1995 ECK Worldwide Seminar, Jennifer had a conscious recall of that past life too. It filled in some missing details. In her recall, she saw an early British settlement in America. It was the sixteenth century, and the place was the Roanoke settlement, today in the easternmost part of North Carolina. The family was happy. The husband was a good worker and a conscientious provider, but he was apt to be absentminded and scattered.

The past-life recall was very direct in the secrets it revealed.

The past-life recall was very direct in the secrets it revealed. First, Mark in that lifetime had caused the fire through neglect. He had forgotten to place a protective shield in front of the fireplace, so a spark ignited their home, burning the family.

Second, Mark's father in this lifetime had been

one of their children. His father's intense anger sprang from that lost lifetime. He never forgave Mark for his carelessness, the reason for his father's behavior.

Third, even today Jennifer is afraid that Mark might err in judgment again. She double-checks him to avoid another catastrophe.

Fourth, Mark now understood the reason for his guilt, anger, shame, and fear from the fire then. A spiritual understanding of that past life has given him a new sense of freedom—because he understands why. As a result he is able to open his heart and accept love from others.

A spiritual understanding of that past life has given him a new sense of freedom—because he understands why. As a result he is able to open his heart and accept love from others.

*   *   *

Dreams can also show the ECK-Vidya, ancient science of prophecy.

James had a prophetic dream. Several miles from the Temple of ECK, Wah Z (the Dream Master) showed him a small, rustic building in an open field. The owner had neglected it.

Wah Z said, "See the analogy to the Temple of ECK?"

He pointed out that if the ECK initiates take the ECK teachings for granted and then neglect them, Eckankar will slowly, almost imperceptibly, fade from the public sight until it is no longer noticed. The pages of history will speak of a pretty but quaint oddity, a spiritual teaching that had no real moment in people's lives.

James saw his dream as an important key to secret worlds.

The leaders in ECK must find ways to preserve the uniqueness of the ECK teachings. Otherwise, they will disappear.

Let's not lose this key to the secret worlds.

9

Yes, Aesop's Animal Stories Still Speak to Us Today

*D*o you want to unfold spiritually?

If that's your aim in reading about experiences with the Light and Sound of God, you may find new inspiration here. You can jump-start your search for truth. Just meet the challenge—open your spiritual eyes.

Some of these ancient truths appear in the animal stories of Aesop, the legendary Greek writer of fables. Animals, too, like maybe your own pets, at times reveal seeds of truth to offer you greater spiritual freedom.

Now let's see what Aesop's fables hold in store spiritually.

Some of these ancient truths appear in the animal stories of Aesop, the legendary Greek writer of fables.

The Young Crab and His Mother

This story teaches the need to set a good example. One day the ungainly, sidewise gait of her young son caught the eye of a mother crab.

"Why, look at how you walk!" she exclaimed.

47

In an effort to make him walk straight, she added, "What kind of walk do you call that?" But her son looked back in bewilderment.

"Show me what you mean, Mother."

"Ah, child!"

Determined to furnish a good example, she set out to show the right way to walk. However, try as she might to turn her toes out, she learned they had an artless habit of pointing in. Of course, this betrayal is due to how crabs are made. They must walk sideways.

So setting a good example tells your children and others who you are and what you believe. It reflects your spiritual light.

Setting a good example tells your children and others who you are and what you believe. It reflects your spiritual light.

The Gnat and the Bull

In a far-off time and place, a tired gnat lit on the tip of a great bull's horn to rest. After he was refreshed, he buzzed down to the bull's ear to shout into it at the top of his miniature voice.

"Thank you, kind Mr. Bull, for letting me catch my breath on your head."

Sleepily, the bull opened his eyes. "Why, I didn't even know you were there."

This fable shows the puffed up self-conceit of some people, who place a lot of weight upon their own importance. Vanity is a terrible block to spiritual progress. So they remain in the dark about the secrets of life and true freedom.

More's the pity.

The Bear and the Bees

Anger is a negative trait, a bad habit that often brings injury and grief to others, though sometimes only to the person who's lost control.

Forgiveness and tolerance are two qualities to help keep one's flash point in check.

Watch, in this story, how a more placid response to an unexpected change in the bear's plans could have made all the difference to the outcome.

*   *   *

Deep in a forest a hungry bear came upon a fallen tree in which honeybees had a gratifying stash of honey. Delighted by his good fortune, he still approached the tree with caution.

Was the swarm of bees at home?

Before he could determine the answer a solitary bee, arriving from a clover field, saw this lumbering thief and stung him.

The bear went into a wild rage.

Attacking the fallen tree with tooth and claw, in an ill-conceived passion to taste the fragrant honey inside, he merely roused the bees. A swarm of hundreds streamed forth. With their own stirred anger, the honeybees stung him over and over.

The bear ran for his life. Only a nearby pool of deep water saved him, for he dove into it to save his skin. His quick action spared him the pain and indignity of countless other stings.

What lesson does this fable of Aesop teach us?

Isn't it usually the wiser course to bridle one's anger over a trifling injury than to risk a thousand more?

The Wolf and the House Dog

In this final parable, Aesop tells of freedom.

One who searches for truth harbors a deep longing for spiritual freedom, the noblest treasure yet

Forgiveness and tolerance are two qualities to help keep one's flash point in check.

known to man. His search is like an unquenchable thirst. It is similar to the distress of a sailor lost at sea in a lifeboat. In his desire for water, he drinks from the ocean. His thirst then becomes like a demon.

A seeker after truth finds its quest the beginning and end of his entire existence.

One who searches for truth harbors a deep longing for spiritual freedom, the noblest treasure yet known to man.

The taste of a little freedom, like honey, directs his cravings toward finding more of it. He will stop at nothing to secure it. The seeker may eventually go so far as to deliberately avoid the company of people who mainly see comfort and luxury as the chief pursuits in life.

So let's hear Aesop's last tale for the day.

*   *   *

Long ago, in a magical land where animals act and talk like people, a wolf went for a stroll. His ribs showed under his matted coat of shabby hair. He tried to ignore his growling stomach.

The town dogs were the reason for his wasted condition, for they were the ruthless, ever-watchful guardians of the town's sheep. These dogs had made him miss many a feast. How he drooled for fat mutton.

To his surprise there happened along one of the sleek, yet fit, town dogs, who looked far too robust to risk an attempt to devour him. So the wolf put on his best face. Flattery was one of his arts. He'd do anything to get those sheep.

"What a fine coat of hair you have," the wolf said. "And how your muscles ripple. You must be the most handsome dog in the whole county."

The dog loved the compliments, so he fell in alongside the wolf and the two engaged in agreeable conversation. "Come, live in town," urged the dog. "It's a splendid life. There's choice food every day of delicious bones, tidbits from the master's table, and even bread and gravy sometimes. The food is served in a bowl. There's no need to chase about in the forest, uncertain of where the next meal will come from. And we get lots of kind words and caresses."

The wolf's ears perked up.

"But what do you have to do to earn all those comforts and luxuries?" he asked.

"Hardly a thing," his companion answered him. "I chase away people when the master's family is out of town, scare vagrants silly, and protect the master's flock."

But then the wolf noticed some hair chafed away on the dog's neck. "What's that mark from?" he asked.

The dog glanced away, suddenly ill at ease.

"That's just the place I wear my collar," he explained. "A chain fastens to it."

Alarmed, the wolf replied, "You mean you don't always run free?"

"Well, not always," the dog admitted. "But it's a small price to pay for all the advantages."

The wolf had heard enough. Bounding to the forest, he cried over his shoulder, "All the sheep in the world aren't worth a single hour of my freedom."

*   *   *

His desire for freedom was like that of a rightful seeker after the mysteries of heaven.

The teachings of ECK can assist you on your own journey of self-discovery on the way to spiritual freedom. They have helped thousands in their quest. The main benefit of the ECK teachings is how you learn to open your heart to God's love.

The main benefit of the ECK teachings is how you learn to open your heart to God's love.

Mark Twain, the renowned American writer, once said, "Keep away from people who try to belittle your ambitions. Small people always do that, but the really great make you feel that you, too, can become great."

The ECK teachings are here for people just like you.

 ### Spiritual Exercise: The Mountain of God

Find a quiet place where no one will disturb you for ten or fifteen minutes. Then shut your eyes and look at a place just above and between the eyebrows. That is the location of the Spiritual Eye.

Now imagine you are climbing to the top of a broad green mountain. Follow the brown dirt path to a meadow of colorful flowers. Powder white clouds near the summit of the mountain give a feeling of great joy, wonder, and freedom. This is the Mountain of God.

When you reach the top, lie down upon the thick, soft carpet of grass. Feel the sunshine warm your face, arms, and body. Shut your eyes there too, as you did when you began this exercise in your room. For the moment, expect complete darkness of the inner vision.

Now look gently for the Light of God to appear in your Spiritual Eye. It may appear in a number of ways. It may come as a soft field of light, similar to the fluffy white clouds near the mountaintop. Again, It may be a pinpoint of light: blue, white, yellow, purple, or even green or pink.

Look gently for the Light of God to appear in your Spiritual Eye. It may appear in a number of ways.

While looking for the Light, softly sing HU over and over again. It is Soul's love song to God. Without staring, continue to watch for the Light within your Spiritual Eye. Listen also for the Sound.

The Sound of God is the vibration of Divine Spirit moving the atoms of life. You may hear the sound of a flute, a rushing wind, the chirping of birds, a waterfall, bells, or the buzzing of bees. These are actual, not imaginary, sounds.

Return to the Mountain of God for a few minutes every day. That journey in contemplation is one of the surest ways to find divine love.

While looking for the Light, softly sing HU over and over again.

The purpose of the ECK teachings is to show you how to be the master of your own life.

CHAPTER THREE

Your Growth in ECK

10
Will Your Love Grow?

*M*any years ago, the ECK gave me a look at what the future would hold should I complete my training and become the spiritual leader of Eckankar. I trembled for days afterward. Nevertheless, the ECK drew me on, past my fears and misgivings.

It gives many updates. Around twelve years ago or more, the ECK-Vidya opened to reveal some important changes that needed to occur over time in how the Mahanta, the Living ECK Master would relate to the ECK initiates as the Outer Master. He would turn over more of the Vahana duties to competent ECK initiates. The Master would make fewer public appearances.

When I mentioned a little of this vision to a few Higher Initiates, their reaction was to recoil in alarm. "Oh, that wouldn't work now," they said.

"Of course not, not now," I reassured them. "Later."

My schedule as the Outer Master was packed for many years with travel, meetings, a host of seminars, trainings, and a lot of writing besides. How would the ECK ever change such a demanding schedule? Easy.

The incredible workload took an inevitable toll on my health. Gradually, my schedule had to be cut back. And back.

One of my favorite quotations from the New Testament is by Paul in a letter to the Philippians. (He wrote wisdom notes too.) To them, he says, "For I have learned, in whatsoever state I am, therewith to be content."

Mark the words: "I have learned." They mean that he had to get used to the new conditions about him too. Each time some outer circumstance arose and changed the way he had been in the habit of doing things, he learned to be content with the will of the Holy Spirit. The same love and trust in the ECK, Divine Spirit, goes for me.

And it should also for you.

In the very earliest days and years of Eckankar, the focus of the ECK teachings drew in very tightly to the Outer Master. Paul Twitchell knew that the majority of chelas did not yet have the spiritual unfoldment to accept at heart and in their very being a master other than Christ. Yes, many people in Eckankar still had some strong ties to the faith of their childhood. Their background was in large part Christian.

As time passed, however, a spiritual maturity began to bring stability to the ranks of the ECK members. More of them grew in discrimination. With a growing trust in the Mahanta, the Inner Master, they could better tell what was ECK and what was not. These individuals came into positions of ECK leadership.

They learned to work with the Eckankar Spiritual Center. They learned the necessity of coordinating their missionary and teaching efforts with

Each time some outer circumstance arose and changed the way he had been in the habit of doing things, he learned to be content with the will of the Holy Spirit.

those of the Mahanta, the Living ECK Master.

After all, it was the Master who instructed the ECK staff.

He helped them create guidelines and keep them current with the rapid changes that occur in a worldwide society. We are in nearly every country in the world. The consciousness in this or that part of the world jumps forward, but then, adverse conditions, set into motion by the Kal, the negative power, try to offset the gains. The Master knows, and watches over, all.

My public appearances, due to health matters, will thus be fewer in the future. It is a necessary step in your spiritual unfoldment. Yet now the chance to become a Co-worker with the Mahanta also increases in like proportion.

This next stage will test your faith in ECK. Will your love grow?

There is a beautiful scene in *The Count of Monte Cristo* by Alexandre Dumas. A young man, Edmond Dantès, is thrown into prison for life because of false accusations by some acquaintances and the self-serving ambitions of a public prosecutor who is corrupt. Years pass for Dantès in a dungeon. Years without hope.

One day, there is an accidental meeting of tunnels for escape. Both Dantès and another prisoner, in solitary confinement for an even longer time, the abbé Faria, have been burrowing toward freedom. But a look out of Dantès' cell window convinces Faria that a tunnel is hopeless. So they become friends. A deep bond develops between Dantès, the young sailor, and the abbé, a man of court and of letters.

Faria undertakes the education of Dantès.

A deep bond develops between Dantès, the young sailor, and the abbé, a man of court and of letters.

New worlds open to the largely unlettered young seaman. Faria, over the years, teaches him the sciences of the day, several languages, a wealth of history and religion. Time passes agreeably for both.

One day the older man senses that they might someday in the near future be parted. That Faria would be moved from his cell. This thought is devastation itself to Dantès, who loves him like his own father. Faria tries to console him. Whoever occupies his cell next, he says, whether young man or old, educated or not, with him Dantès can form a new friendship. Then he can become the teacher. Dantès, now as educated and courtly in deed and manner as his foster father, can pass along this wealth of knowledge to someone else. It would be very useful should liberty ever come.

Dantès is a humble youth. He simply loves the old man and wants nothing more.

After more time elapses, and more tests on loyalty, love, and humility, Faria reveals to Dantès for the first time an unbelievable secret. The abbé knows the location of a fabulous treasure, which he offers to share equally with Dantès, a son truly made in his own image.

In ECK, the Mahanta, the Living ECK Master offers each of you a priceless treasure too. Only this one is a spiritual treasure.

In ECK, the Mahanta, the Living ECK Master offers each of you a priceless treasure too. Only this one is a spiritual treasure.

But you must prove worthy of it. The Master and life itself will test your humility, your love and loyalty to the Sugmad and ECK. Precious jewels of insight lie scattered along the way and will lead you, by your own path and in your own time, to the secrets of God-Realization.

11
From Ashes to Cathedral

Our character develops less from our wins than losses.

My whole life, as yours too, has seen its share of both, but on the whole they made us what we are. Ashes presume a thing was burned. And so it was. That "thing" can include our fondest dreams, plans, and projects.

Yet from the rubble amid smoking ashes we salvage bits and pieces of substances that fire could not consume. Searching about, we also collect new raw materials.

And then, we begin anew on our cathedral of ECK Mastership.

* * *

As a student in high school and college, I felt like a ship without a rudder. Yet the process of spiritual unfoldment was in the works, but on a broader scale than the puny sweep of my vision. So I regarded myself as a failure though in the midst of success.

The ECK Masters were busy, nonetheless, prompting me to accept small roles of leadership, then shed them for larger ones. Step-by-step I built on.

To give service to others is the heart of service

As a student in high school and college, I felt like a ship without a rudder. Yet the process of spiritual unfoldment was in the works.

61

to God as a servant of life. But I never made such
a connection with my first major role of service as
a high-school junior. The job? I was a dining-hall
checker. Our school was on a government milk
program. It received a certain amount of money for
every student who ate a meal in the school's cafete-
ria each month.

A checker's job was to check in all students at
every meal. Two doors led into the dining hall.
Students with names from *A* to *M* charged through
the one door; *N* to *Z* bolted through the other.

Boys and young men from ages fourteen to
nineteen abound in energy and impatience.

A student was to give his five-digit number or
name. A checker then put a check next to that entry.

But hungry students did not stand on ceremony.
They were apt to stampede past the checker's desk,
throwing an inaudible number over their shoulder.
The checker then gave a shout to stop. Sometimes
the student would. Half the time, he galloped up to
the serving line to fix hungry eyes upon the food
awaiting an impatient stomach.

It took a great deal of courage in this six-year
seminary to approach an upperclassman and request his number. I dreaded that part. But in time
I learned graceful ways to make the request and
spare myself retaliation outside my realm of security in the dining hall. Leadership in the making.

Three years later, as a sophomore in college, the
dean of students made me chairman of the dining-
hall committee.

It now was my responsibility to set the checkers'
work schedules, enforce student dress codes, and
keep peace between the students, cooking staff, and
the dean. All done among some five hundred stu-

*It took a great
deal of courage
in this six-year
seminary to
approach an
upperclassman.*

dents. It was like trying to herd a bunch of cats.

Or so it seemed. Yet the leadership role was teaching me how to stand on principle—most of the time. Other occasions demand the wisdom to do nothing.

There was always a trade-off.

Once a group of eight classmates did not like the main dish at supper—macaroni and cheese. It was burned and tough. They made a dismal study of the burnt offering on their plates, then piled all eight servings in a heap on a big serving dish in the middle of the table.

This structure drew the admiration of students at neighboring tables, and they came to see it and stayed to laugh. I shared in their disgust of the meal. Duty called, however.

The place was on the verge of a riot. Heavy in heart, I approached the table. A quiet request to cease and desist, to my surprise, was met with immediate compliance. My cousin and his friends, the school's top athletes and scholars, carried their dishes to the disposal window, then left. No doubt it was to order pizzas. I felt like a hypocrite.

I served as the dining-hall chairman for only a half year then gave my resignation to the dean. It happened like this:

One evening, another group of students would not stomach the food. They were top students, but underclassmen. A near-riot came of the scene. I told Jim, the ringleader, to come to my room at a certain time to discuss the matter. At the appointed hour, I returned to my dorm to find the hallway outside my room lined with Jim's friends.

Outrage rose in their voices. How could the school feed garbage to people?

The leadership role was teaching me how to stand on principle—most of the time. Other occasions demand the wisdom to do nothing.

I beckoned Jim to follow me into my room, half expecting his buddies to push in behind us. That would then have been a serious matter for the dean to handle, but to my wonder, they let the door shut them out.

Jim was a good guy who'd done a stupid thing. The food was good in general. Besides, there was a variety of it. One had but to exercise choice. So he learned.

I put him on table cleanup duty for a week after the evening meals, but he didn't show up once. Wisdom said to leave the situation alone. He'd learned a lesson. Hence I did not pursue him to fulfill his duty, and neither he nor his friends ever made trouble in the dining hall again. Yet I felt a failure for not following up and insisting he do his full punishment.

Soon after, I made an appointment with the dean, who was as tough as any of my training instructors during military service.

He listened to my request to resign. "Why?" he asked.

My roommate had connections to a paying job to help our school in a major fund-raising drive. I was offered it. The dean nodded his approval. He knew better than I that my service as dining-hall chairman had been exemplary. He also saw that the new job was an avenue to more personal growth.

So seeming failures of this kind weren't failures at all. They were rather ashes from which to resume work on my cathedral of ECK Mastership.

You, too, are building a cathedral. Your wins and losses net out to spiritual gains. Stick with the Spiritual Exercises of ECK.

You, too, are building a cathedral. Your wins and losses net out to spiritual gains.

12
Purification by Initiation

A divine power surrounds the time of every ECK initiation. ECKists then often notice a departure from the usual course of events and wonder about the reason behind it.

An ECK initiation has great significance. The hardships some see then are from their agreement with Divine Spirit to move on to a new, higher state of consciousness. They show this agreement by receiving and studying the ECK discourses, which the Mahanta, the Living ECK Master offers them. Sometimes there's a stepped-up current that touches their everyday lives.

What is the point of this spiritual current? It is a love-gift. It purifies Soul.

Here follows the story of an ECKist who reports the dramatic event that occurred the very day the Eckankar Spiritual Center in Minneapolis mailed a pink slip for his Fourth Initiation.

All names in this article are changed to protect people's privacy.

James, from Nigeria, lives in a village nestled at the edge of a large forest. One day, a very spectacular event occurred: there was an attack on his village by a neighboring one.

65

He fled into the bush to save his life. But he soon lost his way.

For two days and nights, James wandered in that thick forest, lost and alone, worried about the fate of family, friends, and neighbors. And what forest is there without poisonous snakes or insects and wild animals? Great dangers were all around. He was afraid.

Meanwhile, a pink slip for his initiation was en route to him.

This was surely a dark night of Soul, a time of great tribulation. And it was then that his thoughts turned to the Mahanta, the Inner Master. So James began to sing HU, that ancient prayer to God. And in that darkest hour of desperation, he wished for assurance of the Master's love and care.

Where was the Master?

"When I needed your company most," says James, "I physically saw an army numbering over a battalion, riding on horseback toward me."

He lost all fear. He knew he was not alone.

When dawn broke he was neither hungry nor thirsty. James set out with confidence, looking for a road to take him home. The paved road he stumbled on led to a distant village. Friendly people gave him directions to his own village, which he reached around nine o'clock that evening.

His family, friends, and neighbors were jubilant at his safe return. Nearly half the villagers had taken refuge in his home and so survived the attack by government militia from the other village.

This incident held three lessons for him. First, he says, "No chela of the Master is ever alone." Second, the Master knew of the grave danger that would have befallen him had he lingered to see the

"When I needed your company most," says James, "I physically saw an army numbering over a battalion, riding on horseback toward me."

outcome of the attack. His eldest brother's son had been shot dead; James would have been shot too. Third, this dark night of Soul was a way to purify him for the higher responsibilities to accompany his Fourth Initiation.

*   *   *

Purification may come in yet other ways. Paul, from West Africa, tells of an inner experience that followed his usual spiritual exercise one night.

Paul is likewise from Nigeria. He reports a dream before his Second Initiation in which the Inner Master purified him of old karma. After the purification Paul's body felt noticeably lighter.

He'd awakened in that life-changing dream to see himself sitting on a chair in his room. Then a bright light, like a full moon, appeared; but it was far too bright to look at.

This was the Light of God. It moved to a position about ten feet above his head. Heat radiated from It. But when it became too intense for his comfort, It would move up higher until the discomfort was much less. The Light continued to adjust Itself up and down. When there was no more heat, a wonderful thing took place. It swirled on to the inner parts of his body.

Here, again, Paul felt a spiritual purification occur. There was some pain at times, to be sure, but the Light of God immediately adjusted Itself to soften the mild unease.

How did Paul perceive this spiritual cleansing?

He saw substances, bad karma, dropping from his body "like a hail of stones." Yes, he felt the pain of this purifying Light. Yet he wanted the dream experience to continue, because his body was vibrating with a wonderful power and love.

In that life-changing dream Paul felt a spiritual purification occur. He saw substances, bad karma, dropping from his body "like a hail of stones."

But then his dream came to an end.

Paul was still vibrating from his experience when he noticed his body felt remarkably light. The Master and the Divine Light had burned off Paul's old karma.

Soon after that came his Second Initiation.

*   *   *

He noticed his body felt remarkably light. The Master and the Divine Light had burned off Paul's old karma.

Helen's story tells of her purification before an ECK initiation too. Here's what happened:

She was at an ECK meeting, and ECKists were asked to sign up for a volunteer project the next day. Twice Helen took up a pen to do so. And twice an inner voice had said, "No!"—the second time quite forcefully. So she turned the matter over to the ECK (Holy Spirit).

The next day was not a normal day in that her family usually left home early and she had the place to herself. Not that morning. Her eighteen-year-old daughter, generally on her way to school by 6:30, lingered, looking for one thing or another in every part of the house until it was very late. Finally, Helen lost her temper. She shouted at her to be off to school; then she stormed into the kitchen to boil a pot of water.

The next instant, Helen came to on the floor. A coal pot with fire and a pan of boiling water were all over her. She screamed for help.

Her daughter, still at home, gave immediate first aid that saved Helen's life. A neighbor, a nurse, tended Helen's burns on her own time, so there were no hospital bills to speak of. The Mahanta had everyone in the right place beforehand. Helen's burns healed unbelievably fast.

A pink slip for Helen's next initiation arrived soon after.

So never waste pity on someone's trials in ECK. They are the Master's gift of love. They purify the ECK initiate, to prepare him for a greater state of spiritual consciousness. That is what it's all about.

Be assured, too, that few purification experiences are as striking as the three mentioned in this article.

Trials in ECK are the Master's gift of love.

13
One Small Change

Things left undone. Huh? What sort of a "how do you do" is that for a spiritual article?

It's like this. Look around. Is life going so fast it's passing you by? Well, dear heart, you have plenty of company. Everybody is running. But is it only a mad rush for the last flight to Endsville?

Slow down and enjoy a walk.

Make one small change and sort through all your activities. It's time to leave some things undone. Just the least important ones, of course. Your life is what you've made it. So drop anger, for example. And self-deception.

Stop and think a minute. Contemplate. What does it all boil down to? (Aren't dry clichés fun?)

A dear friend decided to write his monthly spiritual report for the Master (for himself, really). The past month was loaded with deep inner and outer experiences. But the Mahanta had a better idea. Keep it simple. Talk about love, he said, because love is behind all your experiences anyway.

So Robert, our friend, kept his report simple. He left out less important details.

A long-standing problem with digestion had caused him a lot of discomfort, and the problem was right there every day. Then a light clicked on in his head (and stomach).

"Chew more slowly," said the Mahanta, the Inner Master.

A light clicked on in his head (and stomach). "Chew more slowly," said the Mahanta, the Inner Master.

What? Well, yes, Robert thought over his eating habits: stuff, stuff, shove, shove, jam it down the hole. (My words—certainly not his.) As a matter of fact, Robert thought, he did rather bolt his food.

One small change: he'd chew more carefully.

It seemed a reasonable thing to do: chew his food more slowly. There's still more to his digestive problem, but this change in something so basic as his chewing habit is a boost to his digestion. A small but important change, indeed. What good had all the supplements and vitamins done on top of an unchewed meal? Very little, for sure.

This idea of "one small change" may apply to other areas of his life too, Robert suspects. And it does.

Perhaps it also means anchoring his love in the Mahanta, the Living ECK Master, on the face of the faceless ECK (the Holy Spirit). Yet how?

By finding and opening the inner door with the Spiritual Exercises of ECK and through self-love. Then, balancing the inflow of God's love through love and service to others. That's the lesson Robert learned as he was gathering his thoughts for his monthly initiate report to the Master.

*   *   *

Then there's the case of Ned (not his real name).

A member of Eckankar these many years, Ned had some personal hang-ups. But like many, he tried to pin them on others, because it's easier on one's self-image.

The source of his hang-ups (inner turmoil) was

anger. An old friend, that mental passion. Finally, after a few jolts in his everyday life, he realized his anger was really directed at the Mahanta, the Living ECK Master. It was over a difference of opinion about the true direction of Eckankar.

(On the Master's part: no hard feelings. Such bumps go with the turf.)

Ned, however, had a lot going for him spiritually, so the ECK Masters decided he was worth the trouble of softening up.

The first jolt occurred at work.

By trade Ned is a book designer, and a good one. Then came a series of rude awakenings where he needed to change a design more than once. Sometimes it was at the request of the author, the editor, or even an artist who had nothing to do with the project. Ned became angry.

It was only a spiritual test. The ECK Masters wanted to see whether he had the honesty to look at himself and his creation, the book's design.

He did. Ned looked at the suggested corrections and knew they improved his original concept. It took a big man to admit it. One small change.

A hurdle cleared.

Then, on a visit home, his younger brother told some family stories. He remarked, "You were always extremely stubborn, Ned." (No, not him. Ned didn't recall that streak of stubbornness.) So jolt number two—and a second hurdle cleared because he knew it was true.

He got to thinking. After a talk by the Mahanta, the Living ECK Master at a recent seminar on the gifts of the Holy Spirit all around, the idea finally penetrated the fog clouding his mind. Ned realized that over the years he'd considered the Master a

Ned looked at the suggested corrections and knew they improved his original concept. It took a big man to admit it. One small change.

wimp. The Master seemed like a ninety-seven-pound weakling to him.

(Ah, well, no hard feelings from the Master. He's been accused of worse.)

Ned was willing to reconsider that opinion and others, because he wanted to enjoy the abundant gifts of the ECK all around him. But anger had shut them out.

So he made a small change in there somewhere (in his heart).

A third hurdle cleared, and the ECK Masters nodded in approval. So Rebazar Tarzs, an ECK Master, came to Ned in a dream. "Come here, Ned. Come here, Ned." He heard himself reply in wonder, "Yes, Rebazar?"

The great ECK Master Rebazar Tarzs would actually try to work with him in the dream state? It left Ned in a very humble state of mind. One small change.

Since then he's made some big changes, becoming active with the ECK missionary work again, a source of much joy in years gone by. The result is a renewed interest in living. New people are actually finding the teachings of ECK due to his love and service to the Holy Spirit. And all because Ned was willing to be honest with himself.

*   *   *

The two people mentioned above showed honesty about issues sensitive to them. Only then could they make the necessary changes. Just one small change at a time.

So leave the useless things alone. For, after all, those are blocks to reaching a happier and richer state of spiritual consciousness. You deserve better, don't you?

Ned was willing to reconsider that opinion and others, because he wanted to enjoy the abundant gifts of the ECK all around him.

14
Paul Twitchell in Context of the Times

*I*n 1964 and 1965, Paul Twitchell's state of consciousness was in fluctuation. At times he seemed very near the Mahantaship, which he was to receive on October 22, 1965.

But he did drift back and forth in consciousness. There were still signs of Paul's failure to yet see and know the fullness of the divine plan for Soul's education.

Paul, then, is a perfect example of the seesawing that Soul goes through in Its aspirations for the Oneness of All Being. It is as the doctor said of a patient: "Yesterday he was better, but today he is worse!" Finally, however, the patient does make a full recovery. In the end, Paul does become the Mahanta, the Living ECK Master. His struggles for Mastership did come to a fitting conclusion.

It might be awkward for us to accept this frailty of consciousness in Paul unless we acknowledge the principle that he and all beings—even the Mahanta in training—undergo marked changes in perception as their unfoldment progresses.

Paul is a perfect example of the seesawing that Soul goes through in Its aspirations for the Oneness of All Being.

The saving grace in Eckankar is that absolute perfection is outside the context of an unfinished and expanding creation. That is exactly the nature of the true God Worlds. Soul may reach the canopy of heaven, but that canopy opens to a still more majestic creation beyond it.

By and large, Paul wrote for the people of his times. This was necessarily so because the Mahanta, the Living ECK Master responds to the spiritual conditions that prevail during his term of service to God. As the human race expands in consciousness to even the smallest degree, it calls for a like adjustment in the outer teachings of ECK. Therefore, the written and spoken works of ECK are suited exactly to the temper of the times in which they are given.

As the world society has an expansion of awareness, the Living ECK Master adapts the eternal teachings from the inner planes to match the spiritual needs of his audience.

At one point in his preparation for the ECK Mastership, Paul criticized the Catholic Church for making itself the beneficiary of the apostolic tradition. But despite the attempts at reform in Vatican II, it had long before that become a crystallized social religion. The life had already gone out of the primitive Christian church itself when Christ left it in the hands of a committee of apostles.

His retirement as the leader of the new religion caused it to lose much of the dynamic expression of the Life Force.

The church stumbled along in its evolution, fighting schism, until there was no alternative but to create a more unified leadership role than "Church Father." That was the ecclesiastical office that re-

By and large, Paul wrote for the people of his times.

placed the authority of the apostles. In AD 590, the Roman Catholic Church came to accept its first pope, Gregory I. The church leaders saw the need for a strong, worldly-wise head if the church was to survive. But neither the first pope nor any of his successors had the power of the Word—the Light and Sound of God.

The main difference between Eckankar and all other religions is that the Mahanta, the Living ECK Master is the Word. He is the ECK.

The survival of a religion depends upon more than miracles and prophecy. Both were a strong part of the early Christian church until at least AD 200. But the church's real loss at the death of Christ was that no living individual could replace him as its inner and outer master.

Once the light of spirituality is lit in a new religion, it must be tended every moment. Otherwise, the divine fire begins to flicker and go out. The life-giving spiritual element quickly gives way to formalism.

For a while, the Christian church was invigorated by prophecies of Christ's Second Coming. But as time passed and he did not reappear, the internal discipline of the early church grew lax. In reaction, the laxness in conduct sprouted heretical groups, such as Montanism. This schismatic group of the late second century renewed prophecies of the Second Coming, while entering into a strict ascetic life.

The interesting thing about the prophecies of the Second Coming is that they express Christianity's unconscious need for a living master. The people's hope of Christ's return is the cement that holds the church together. Yet in Luke 9:27, Jesus says, "But I tell you of a truth, there be some standing here, which

The main difference between Eckankar and all other religions is that the Mahanta, the Living ECK Master is the Word. He is the ECK.

shall not taste of death, till they see the kingdom of God."

However, when Jesus spoke of this Kingdom of God, he was not speaking of his physical return but of a spiritual awakening. He made it most clear where and when the Kingdom of God would come.

While some in Christ's time would actually witness the Kingdom of God, most would not. Christ spoke truth, but few in organized faith knew what he meant. That misunderstanding has carried forward even to the present day. Seeing the Kingdom of God is an individual matter that depends upon the unfoldment of each person. It will not be a global event of one time or place. Christ explained the coming of the Kingdom of God quite clearly.

When the Pharisees asked Christ, in Luke 17:20, when the Kingdom of God should come, he answers, "The kingdom of God cometh not with observation: Neither shall they say, Lo here! or, lo there! for, behold, the kingdom of God is within you."

The apostles are long gone, yet today's Christians still look outside themselves for the Kingdom of God.

*   *   *

The writings of Paul Twitchell will be available for years to come, but they will always be secondary to the message of the Living ECK Master of the times.

The writings of Paul Twitchell will be available for years to come, but they will always be secondary to the message of the Living ECK Master of the times. This is the edge that Eckankar has over Christianity. The Sound and Light of God are embodied in the Mahanta, the Living ECK Master. He—through the Sound and Light—can lead Soul to victory over death and reincarnation.

The spiritual evolution of mankind goes ever forward. A Second Initiate from Paul's day would be several notches lower in consciousness than a

Second Initiate in ECK today. This spiral of evolution includes even the Mahantaship, which is part of the unfinished creation of Sugmad. As hard as it may be to imagine, the newest full Mahanta always starts his term with a greater level of consciousness than ever existed in a previous era of history.

The lover of truth is reminded that he is Soul. He exists because God loves him. If dream travel, Soul Travel, and experiences in the Sound and Light of ECK are to accomplish anything, it is this: the individual's realization of infinite love.

Pure love is what Soul is always seeking. It is as Rebazar Tarzs says to the seeker in *Stranger by the River*: "Love is most sublime, having its origin in the House of God. In whatever heart love blooms, that Soul will be lifted and carried to the highest abode of the Supreme Sugmad."

So love ever the Sugmad (God), the ECK (Holy Spirit), and the Mahanta (the Inner Messenger). Then all will be spiritually well with you.

Pure love is what Soul is always seeking.

15
Wannabe Prophets, Dream Analysts, and Other Guides

*J*udging by my mail, some people would love to set themselves up in business as spiritual consultants to others. Easy life, easy money.

They are wannabes, often vain and lazy people who are looking for an easy way to make a living. What about service to God and mankind? (Huh?) A wannabe is someone who *wants to be* someone he's not, for all the glory it will bring him.

A boy watching TV sees American basketball star Michael Jordan and says, "I wanna be like Michael Jordan." Instead of keeping his dream to himself, then going outside to give his dream a chance by shooting baskets, he flips channels and watches more TV. He'll never be a star.

There are wannabes for nearly every high-profile profession. That is especially true if a certain field doesn't require a degree, certificate, or license. Then it must be easy.

Lots of things are easy if poorly done. That's why someone who truly loves God will do every-

A wannabe is someone who wants to be someone he's not, for all the glory it will bring him.

thing for the sheer love of it. Anything done for love must be the very best that an individual can do, no matter how humble the task or undertaking.

Wannabes are really attracted to the field of spiritual guidance. ("Ah, the fame, the fortune, the opportunity!" Those are their sometimes not-so-secret thoughts.)

The prophet field is very attractive. But it's usually the most difficult to achieve in, because it requires a bit of knowledge in some other field, and some public success, before people will even give a wannabe a hearing. So it's popular with people in the health field.

Today, without looking very hard, it's possible to find a popular author of health or self-help books who is throwing out feelers to his readers about becoming their spiritual guide. That's not to say this is wrong. True messengers of God come from all sorts of backgrounds, even the most humble. Consider Jesus, the carpenter's son.

There was also Martin Luther, the Protestant reformer. His father was a miner.

My father was a farmer.

A true spiritual guide has often led a hard, exacting life in some way. While someone like the young man who later became the Buddha began life in the lap of luxury, it was an extreme contrast to the life he eventually found outside the sheltered walls of his youth. The resultant shock opened his eyes to his mission of service to others.

Each individual who reaches mastership has gone through many trials by fire and water.

Each individual who reaches mastership has gone through many trials by fire and water. And life doesn't get easy later.

Dreams also attract people who would like to become well known as dream analysts through their books, articles, or talks before groups. Many books on dream symbols are honest attempts to add to the pool of knowledge on dreams. However, a wannabe tries a shortcut. Not much of a dreamer himself, he reads a lot of books on dreams and then writes his own with a particular slant. Anything to catch the public's eye.

Anything to make easy money.

Many books on dreams do a disservice to the readers. The books will give a list of symbols like an eagle, key, car, house, flower, person, etc., and say it means a certain thing. It's the most narrow interpretation of dreams possible.

Dreams are about you. Each dream must be taken in the context of what you're doing, feeling, hoping, or fearing—now. In Eckankar, an individual gets a lot of help from the Mahanta, the Living ECK Master. He is the Outer and Inner Master. He has the spiritual power. So among other roles like the Wayshower, he is also the Dream Master.

One of the marks of a true Master is his ability to teach people outwardly. (Many wannabes can write books, articles, or give talks.)

Yet a true Master will also teach his students inwardly. (Not too many wannabes can do that.)

My files at Eckankar have countless testimonials from people who are learning to interpret their own dreams. No one is better suited to interpret your dreams than you. The skill doesn't come overnight. But if people stick with the guidance that the Mahanta, the Living ECK Master gives them, they can become very good interpreters of their own dreams.

Who gives false prophets, poor dream interpreters, and so-called spiritual guides who are charla-

One of the marks of a true Master is his ability to teach people outwardly. Yet a true Master will also teach his students inwardly.

tans their base? The gullible public, no other. It is a human weakness to adore someone who flatters you.

It is a human weakness to adore someone who flatters you.

So these false guides usually pat their followers on the back and maybe chastise them a little at times—but not too much. (It's bad for business.)

Mentioned already was the healer with a growing practice who has visions of moving into the field of spiritual guidance. He mixes remedies, prescriptions, and healing advice with side comments about a patient's past lives. You'd be surprised how a good report on a fantastic past-life history endears the patient to his doctor.

The odd and amusing thing is that the doctor's prescription may be wrong 50–70 percent of the time. However, vitality in a young body can overcome those errors and recover anyway. But children, the very ill, or the elderly are more susceptible to errors in prescription and may face a series of debilitating or life-threatening side effects.

Guess who is more easily taken in by such past-life glimpses—those with a natural vitality or those without?

The very ill and the elderly are most likely to suffer ill effects when half the doctor's remedies are inaccurate and cause them distress. This group ought to be equally cautious about any past-life glimpses from the doctor. If he's wrong half the time in handing out remedies, what should make anyone believe that his past-life insight is any better?

Yet people do. They'll accept excuses or explanations of "healing crisis," just "a dumping of toxins," and the like. They want to believe. It's human nature to want to believe someone in authority: the old parent-child training.

The spiritual leader of Eckankar begins by helping the student. But then he teaches the student to help himself. He does not want or expect people to depend upon him for things they could better do themselves.

Like interpreting their dreams. Like learning how to tell whether a consultant—dream, health, legal, or spiritual—is a charlatan or the real thing.

The purpose of the ECK teachings is to show you how to be the master of your own life. That's what you should "wanna be."

The purpose of the ECK teachings is to show you how to be the master of your own life.

 Spiritual Exercise: On the Rooftops

Imagine yourself placing a ladder against the house. Anchor it very securely with ropes, then climb the ladder and sit on the rooftop, staying within reach of the ladder.

Listen for a rushing wind. This is how the ECK, or Holy Spirit, sounds at a certain level when you are listening with the spiritual ears of Soul. Sometimes It comes as a high-energy sound, as though you were standing next to a jet engine, a huge motor, or a dynamo. If you hear It for even a brief time, this is good. It means that the action of the ECK is working in you, purifying and uplifting.

If you're afraid the wind might blow you off the roof, look at it another way: The ECK will blow you into new circumstances in your outer life. As above, so below.

When the sound of the Holy Spirit begins to come through Soul, to purify and cleanse, you can remember the ladder. It's nearby if you need it. Feel secure that you won't be blown off into the dark unknown.

And when the fear subsides, you'll be led into the next step very naturally.

"I heard of your illness and remembered your tears of joy at my songs, so I came," the nightingale replied.

CHAPTER FOUR

Divine Love

16
Our Greatest Teachers

*I*s God's love greater for child or king?

Let's say the child's a beast and the king's a saint, beloved for his just dealings and kindness. Will less sunshine and more rain assail the willful child?

God loves sinner and saint, child and king. Each is Soul, a singular creation, made of God's own Essence. So child and king are equal. Divine love is Soul's birthright. However, the Voice of God does place a cadre of teachers around every individual. These teachers fit the circumstances of the pupil's age, spiritual capacity, and his need to absorb some important lesson of the hour.

Who, then, are these teachers?

People you know well. Over a lifetime this special gathering of teachers may be parents, siblings, or relatives.

The following years will see others too.

Our mates, friends, fellow workers, strangers, and more, all join the march of time. Each is our greatest teacher at some point. Each contributes the exact lesson needed in the moment of giving it. Each teacher and lesson add a dash of color to the

The Voice of God does place a cadre of teachers around every individual. Who, then, are these teachers?

canvas of our own, someday-to-be masterpiece of divine purity.

Rumi, a sage and extraordinary poet of thirteenth-century Persia, is one such great teacher. He was a disciple of the famed Shamus-i-Tabriz, ECK Master. That's why he's of interest here. His voice still rings along the corridors of time.

Its echo still quickens our spirits today.

Rumi tells of a Persian king's teacher on a battlefield. You'll find this story and the two that follow in *This Longing*, a small volume of Rumi's poetry, stories, and letters rendered into brisk and beautiful English by Coleman Barks and John Moyne (Threshold Books, 1988).

A close friend had a quarrel with Husam, Rumi's scribe. For twelve long years, Husam would freely offer his services to record Rumi's huge body of dictated poetry, the *Masnavi* (also, *Mathnawi*). All three, it appears, were boyhood chums. So in a personal letter, Rumi begs the offended one to forgive and forget. Husam always had kind thoughts for the other. He'd never speak ill.

Rumi warns, small misunderstandings grow into big things. Resolve them now. Don't wait.

To make his point, he tells this story:

One of a king's valiant warriors had lost his steed to wounds in battle. The king lent him a horse. It was a favorite Arabian. This horse, too, received injury, and the king's displeasure fell to the warrior. Word of the royal temper flew straight to this loyal soldier like an arrow. He rode to the king and dismounted. Never again would his services benefit this king.

The warrior had not hesitated to risk his life to help the king win this battle, so why the complaints

Rumi is one such great teacher. He was a disciple of the famed Shamus-i-Tabriz, ECK Master.

about wounds to the king's favorite horse?

"I will serve a King who appreciates my soul. I shall take my jewel to One who knows jewels."

The warrior was a hard but fair teacher.

In another letter, Rumi again tells of a king and his teacher on a battlefield. This time the teacher was a dervish, an enlightened one.

Rumi said he could think of no reason he sent this letter to its recipient. Maybe, he suggested, it was to urge him to be generous with his possessions before death snatched them from his hand.

Give what you can, while you can.

"No dead person," he said, "grieves for his own death. He, or she, mourns only what he didn't do. 'Why did I wait? Why did I not . . . ? Why did I neglect to . . . ?' " Rumi offered good spiritual advice.

So, to illustrate the point, he tells this story.

Sultan Mahmood was in India, waging a campaign. Things were going badly. The Indian troops greatly outnumbered his own. Defeat loomed.

In desperation, the king fell to his knees. He prayed to God. He promised to give all spoils of battle to the poor if God would grant him the victory. And against all odds the tide did turn in Mahmood's favor as the enemy troops seemed to wilt before his own men.

But victory posed a dilemma. What should he tell the troops? They expected their cut.

When they heard of his vow to give all spoils to the poor, anger burst from the ranks. "We're the poor," they demanded. "Give the spoils to us."

Cornered, the king looked around for counsel.

It happened just then that a dervish came along. The king called him over for advice.

"What shall I do?" he asked the holy man.

"I will serve a King who appreciates my soul." The warrior was a hard but fair teacher.

"That depends," said the dervish. "Do what your men want—if you'll never seek another favor from God. But keep your battlefield vow if there's a chance you'll ever want God's favor again."

It's still good advice today. So be generous with what you can give to ECK while you remain in control of your goods.

Don't let regrets haunt you later.

Rumi, in a third letter, tells of a close friend, Saladin, who showed family and friends the right way to celebrate his passing from this earth. Saladin, in his will, said his funeral was to be an occasion for rejoicing. He wanted no clouds of sorrow.

So bring on the tambourines, drums, and dancers. Let all be glad, let laughter fill the streets; let others see how those of God return to God. Death is cause to celebrate. Let all show their happiness.

Everyone at the funeral did as Saladin wished. It was a day of dancing, music, and delight.

And so Rumi's friend was the great teacher at his own funeral. Such an air of festivity will someday be at the funerals of ECKists too. It's but a matter of when. We'll feel deep loneliness, of course. Our good-byes will come in private, though, with close friends. Healing the wound of loss takes time. There will be a hollow void in our lives, no doubt; however, with the love and support of near and dear ones, our broken heart will mend.

Here are three lessons to glean from Rumi. These three simple things will bring peace and joy to you.

So here are three lessons to glean from Rumi, one of earth's great teachers—take them to heart. One, be loyal to those who help you. Two, keep your word to God. And three, celebrate the death of one who returns to God.

These three simple things will bring peace and joy to you.

17
God's River of Love

*L*ove is the River of God. It carries all living things upon it toward spiritual perfection.

It shows itself every day, but how many of us know it to be so? Consider the following riddle.

*   *   *

If you were to teach a fish, a duck, and a rattlesnake about water, which would find the concept most difficult?

Most people say the rattlesnake because it uses water the least. However, the fish has the hardest time understanding the concept of water. Why do you suppose? Yes, because it lives within the water itself. The fish is completely immersed in the very environment of which one is trying to make it aware.

The duck, on the other hand, has the most experience with the variety of water. It lives in two worlds, in water and out of it.

The duck meets creatures that live only in the water, only on land, and both in water and on land. The duck drinks water. It lives or nests on land. It swims on water. Yet the duck can also fly above water, letting it make a comparison of above and below.

Love is the River of God. It carries all living things upon it toward spiritual perfection.

From the air, it can see the tracings of the wind upon a lake. Also, it knows the look of rainfall upon a mirrored surface, and the return and sending of the sun's golden sheen.

The duck, in short, has a broad range of experience with water. So the duck would catch the concept of water faster than either the rattlesnake or the fish.

*   *   *

The ECK teachings offer a broad approach so the God seeker may see and experience life's many sides. True stories of ECKists may give you valuable insights on dreams, past lives, Soul Travel, or on life day by day.

The golden thread within the secret teachings of ECK is divine love. It connects all life with the divine Creator.

Love is the why behind a miraculous healing, a gift of protection from danger, or a special communication with loved ones who are dying or have passed on.

Love is the healer, the teacher, the helper, the friend, and yes, the lover of Soul.

One who loves God loves life. This love bestows protection and gratitude upon an individual. One in the mantle of divine love will act with charity toward others, in the most trying ordeals.

One in the mantle of divine love will act with charity toward others, in the most trying ordeals.

Hot Tea

An example is the story of Carolyn. Some years ago she went to a restaurant with family and friends. The waitress asked if they wanted drinks, so Carolyn decided on a glass of ice water. The group enjoyed the meal cooked at the table. Later, the waitress brought a tray with six cups of hot tea for the party.

She tripped. The scalding tea splashed on Carolyn's back. Screaming in pain, she jumped forward. Her thin green silk dress offered little protection.

Carolyn's sister, seated beside her, seized the glass of ice water and threw it on her back.

The scene passed in slow motion for Carolyn. The shocked waitress stood, transfixed in time, a look of horror frozen on her face. The waitress's heart ached for Carolyn.

And Carolyn's heart ached for the waitress.

Carolyn assured her she was OK, not wanting her to feel bad or worry about losing her job. The young woman accompanied her to the washroom, crying for the pain she'd caused.

Carolyn's heart opened wide to her.

A quick check at the hospital revealed only minor burns. The instinctive action of Carolyn's sister had kept the hot tea from doing serious damage.

Many people said to sue. Carolyn rejected the advice, because she saw only love in the face of the kind waitress.

The restaurant sent free meal tickets. It also enclosed waiver forms, freeing it of legal liability. Without a second's hesitation, Carolyn signed and returned the papers.

A year later, she went to the restaurant again. A cook remembered her. "Aren't you the lady who had the hot tea poured down your back?" The cook remarked how amazed the staff had been about how well she took the accident.

Carolyn was in awe. It surprised her they remembered.

The first instinct many people have today in the

Many people said to sue. Carolyn rejected the advice, because she saw only love in the face of the kind waitress.

face of a real or imagined injury is to file a lawsuit. It may be necessary to protect one's own property, but as often is the case, a lawsuit is an excuse to steal another's property.

Why is it so? Could it be that love is missing in a society?

*   *   *

God's River of Love makes its appearance in everyday life, as in Carolyn's hot-tea story above. Yet it shows up in a multitude of other forms. Dreams are a big part of learning for an ECKist.

John's Dream

John grew up in a Roman Catholic and Episcopal background. Then he married Joyce.

She'd been an ECKist for many years, but his training as a scientist made him suspicious of Eckankar and all religions. Along the way, he attended ECK seminars with Joyce and their family. But he felt out of place. He also read some ECK books.

Yet John could not attach so much importance to dreams as Joyce did. He wanted scientific proof.

Then he had this dream.

The couple was expecting their firstborn child. One night, six weeks before the expected date of birth, John met the yet unborn child in a remarkable dream. On parting she said with joy, "Bye-bye, Daddy. See you next week."

John expected another dream meeting in a week.

However, Joyce went into labor then, five weeks early. Their daughter was born hours later. John had his proof about the reality of dreams. He, too, became a member of Eckankar.

Six weeks before the expected date of birth, John met the yet unborn child in a remarkable dream.

Joyce's Dream

The tiny infant, too young to breathe alone, faced days in an incubator in the hospital. Her life hung in the balance.

One night Joyce had a dream with Rebazar Tarzs and a circle of ECK Masters around the child. "Oh, good!" said Joyce, "You're going to heal her!" It was a shock when Rebazar replied, "No."

"Then I will heal her," said Joyce.

He agreed she could. However, he warned, to intervene would break a spiritual law. The child had chosen to enter an unprepared body for an important experience. By right, it was her decision alone whether to stay or go.

The spiritual travelers and the mother gazed upon the child's struggling form. She'd decided to let divine love rule.

Rebazar Tarzs produced a rose from within his maroon robe and laid it upon the tiny girl. The room began to glow with a golden light, connecting the child with the heavens. Joyce then returned to her human body.

The child chose to stay. A few days later the doctors let her go home with her grateful parents.

*   *   *

Such is the power of God's River of Love. It gives nourishment to one and all, whether the gift is seen or not.

Such is the power of God's River of Love. It gives nourishment to one and all, whether the gift is seen or not. It is also like a gentle rain, falling upon both great and small.

Are you seeking truth?

Eckankar offers a unique, individual path to love, wisdom, power, and spiritual freedom. It opens the floodgates of love to all who are worthy of true love.

18
Renovations of the Heart

*E*ach Soul begins life in the material worlds like a spiritual infant. It's completely helpless. With the passage of time and more incarnations, the individual gains in spiritual maturity. Soul unfolds and grows in wisdom.

From an overview, then, the people of the world range in spiritual age from infant to child, to youth, to adult, to the elder, to the very old.

People are known by the company they keep. It's an old adage, but it cuts right to the heart of the matter.

Maybe it ought to be no great surprise to the few of wisdom that so many people around the world choose a corrupt leader for an idol. In their hearts they are like him. All of them, in the whole, show spiritual immaturity.

Aesop tells the fable of the ass who carried an image. See how it applies to spiritual infants and children, yet also understand that they can only behave within the limits of their gained experiences.

A sacred image was to be transported to a temple. The image was strapped to the back of an ass driven by his owner.

Each Soul begins life in the material worlds like a spiritual infant.

What a grand procession!

In the train of the ass bearing the image followed a parade of priests decked out in their finery. As the procession passed crowds of bowing people who lined the streets, the ass thought their reverence was for him. The ass stopped in his tracks to address their homage. He brayed loudly.

But his handler guessed what thoughts had entered the animal's head. He began to hit him with a stick to get him moving again.

"You stupid ass," he shouted. "The honor is for the image, not you!"

Likewise, people who glorify a Kal leader think to assume some of his glory by praising him. Every tyrant in history could boast of supporters. Without them he was nothing.

The teachings of ECK recognize the various spiritual ages among the billions of humanity. People of all levels of maturity come to ECK. But the length of time they stay in ECK depends upon whether they are spiritual children or elders, and all stages of life in between. The immature stop for a sip of the Living Waters of ECK and move on.

Others stay longer.

But simply a long tenure in Eckankar is no way to determine a person's spiritual maturity either. Some infants stay because it takes too much effort to go elsewhere. They stand out because of their tepid, halfhearted support of the Mahanta, the Living ECK Master. Yet he is the teacher. He uses every possible means to help them unfold spiritually too.

The Master's specialty is renovations of the heart.

The Master's specialty is renovations of the heart. For a renewal to occur in the heart, the seeker must allow him to help tear out the old, useless traits and habits. It is difficult for some to let go of past comfortable ways.

One way to advance spiritually is to choose new friends and people to associate with.

George Washington, the first U.S. president, said, "Associate yourself with men of good quality if you esteem your own reputation; for 'tis better to be alone than in bad company."

That's one of many small renovations of the heart.

People who are making important strides include a very humble man who let the Master show him the condition of his heart. Now he sees problems as spiritual blessings. He knows that ECK, the Holy Spirit, gives us challenges to help with spiritual unfoldment.

Here's what he learned:

He set up a business in a new state. Soon clients came for his services, as expected. What he'd not reckoned on, though, was the poor caliber of some clients. These people were out of balance, unhappy, gruff, and opinionated.

Then the Mahanta opened his Spiritual Eye. To his shock, this individual saw that his clients were just a mirror of his own condition.

Our friend has started to see a greater manifestation of Spirit in his everyday life. But he's also learned to see the blessings of life, dressed as challenges, and tries to find creative solutions for them.

Not surprisingly the old, negative clients are dropping away. New ones with clear and bright eyes have replaced them, and he finds it a joy to work with them.

What helped the renovation of his heart?

Our friend has learned to see the blessings of life, dressed as challenges, and tries to find creative solutions for them.

He gives credit to the 15× spiritual exercise the Mahanta, the Living ECK Master wrote about before. It's an easy one. However, it does require some patience and much discipline to make it a habit. One simply writes a few qualities or conditions he'd like to have, like purity, love, health, wealth, joy, and so on. These go into a single sentence. Write, "I am . . ." Use the present tense. Then just write that sentence fifteen times each day.

Thomas Fuller, a clergyman, once said, "He that would have the fruit must climb the tree." In other words, he must do something (the right thing) to get it.

Silas from Nigeria felt he needed a new personal word for his daily contemplations, so he asked the Mahanta for one. Within a day or two, he had a vivid spiritual dream. In the dream Silas saw a mysterious white flood that covered the entire universe. He looked for a place of refuge. Any time, he feared, it would reach and consume him.

Then he awoke.

Immediately, he did a contemplation to understand its meaning. "The great flood is the ECK flooding your consciousness," said the Mahanta.

The ECK is only the Sound and Light of God. It's also the Voice of God, because at the core of every divine messenger and message is God's love in the form of Sound and Light.

But there is more. Silas soon did a spiritual exercise again. In a second dream, he was moving along a path that led to a housing area under construction. Along the path he found a wooden signpost. It appeared to have undergone a renovation. On the board was his current spiritual word.

The meaning was clear. The Mahanta had reno-

He gives credit to the 15× spiritual exercise the Mahanta, the Living ECK Master wrote about before. It's an easy one.

vated his personal word, now charged with new spiritual vitality, so that it would further open his spiritual eye. His contemplations had new life again.

The experiences in life are to help purify the heart. Those who have the eyes to see the divine Light, and the ears to hear the holy Sound, will be blessed with a renovation of their heart.

This promise is good for young and old alike.

The experiences in life are to help purify the heart.

19
Heaven's Narrow Door

A conversation about spiritual matters may start in unexpected ways. One such conversation took place at my eye doctor's office yesterday, the day of my annual eye exam.

The doctor had lost his father earlier this year. In the final weeks of his father's last illness, the doctor had dropped everything on weekends to fly from Minneapolis to Arizona to visit him.

Unexpectedly, he said, "The door to heaven must be narrow."

A twinkle in his eye begged the question, Why?

The doctor and his father had grown very close over the past few years, so death had left a big vacuum in the doctor's life.

"My dad was nearly ninety," he said, "and had been a rather stocky man most his life. But he was very thin when he finally left.

"The same with others I've known," he went on. "So the door to heaven must be very narrow."

We had a laugh about that.

On a more serious note, he recounted the last days of his father. The old man had lived a long, full life, yet he clung eagerly to this life, uncertain about

He said, "The door to heaven must be narrow." A twinkle in his eye begged the question, Why?

what the next had to offer. But as time passed, he began to have inner experiences of a bright white place. Ahead of him in the vision stood a white staircase. It led up to a door.

Yet no matter how hard he tried to get through the door to a new life in the heavenly worlds, he couldn't get it open. It frustrated him to no end.

Then he'd open his eyes in the hospital room, look at his son, and say, "I'm not in heaven yet, am I?"

"How do you know that?" his son asked.

"Because you're still sitting here."

They enjoyed a good laugh.

Then, his father had gone on, happy and content at his good fortune in having mastered the secret to opening the door at the top of the white staircase. However, he left behind a very reflective and lonesome son, the doctor.

"The passing of one's parents can be a traumatic event," I said, addressing his unspoken fear. "It means we're next in line."

He smiled ruefully, relieved that someone had put a handle on the cup for him.

"I'm the clan leader now," he agreed. He seemed to come to terms with his new role.

Then it was on to business. The doctor is a hardworking, gifted man who loves people. On average, he cancels appointments only two or three times a year, but family problems had forced a cancellation of my two previous appointments. He made profuse apologies.

When the eye exam was over, I made as if to get up from the chair, because Joan wanted him to recheck her prescription. The conversation and exam had eaten into his lunch hour, but he seemed grate-

He'd open his eyes in the hospital room, look at his son, and say, "I'm not in heaven yet, am I?" "How do you know that?" his son asked.

ful for two sympathetic listeners. So he waved his hand for me to stay seated a moment more.

"Since you're here," he said, "may I ask you a question? What do you know about parallel worlds?"

The doctor is a Christian; his father was a benevolent agnostic who simply didn't know what to think about the hereafter. He was perfectly satisfied to enjoy the fruits of this life: his wife, family, friends, good health, and profession. His heaven was earth. That's all he could be certain of, and it pleased him.

Our good friend the doctor now felt a desire to know where his father was and how he was doing. Hence, the question about parallel worlds.

"Going into the heavenly worlds while still in the human body is the key to Soul Travel and dream travel," Joan and I said between us. He looked uncertain of how to use either to accomplish his desire of meeting his dad again.

"Love is stronger than fear or even death," I said. "Whenever there is a strong bond of love between two people, they can meet again in their dreams or by Soul Travel."

But the doctor, the Christian, hesitated.

I continued: "A master you trust spiritually, like Christ, can make it happen. Just ask him in your prayers. He can take you to your father in a dream. He'll take care of all the details so you won't have to learn the dream methods yourself."

That agreed with him. An air of tranquillity now settled upon his face. He thought for a moment longer, then smiled. Oh, yes, our eyes were fine.

Many of you have also spoken about the chance, yet very spiritual, conversations that happen to you as you move about day to day. You are then aware

Whenever there is a strong bond of love between two people, they can meet again in their dreams or by Soul Travel.

of the great love of the ECK, the Holy Spirit. It cares so much for each wandering Soul that It arranges a way to bring more light, love, and knowledge to all who ask for it in a spirit of childlike innocence. And often through you.

Heaven's narrow door?

Yes, an individual must indeed leave behind all attachment to the things of this world before it's possible to go through heaven's door.

Abandon all things but one.

Pure love.

It is the key that opens the door to the *highest* place in heaven—God's home of Love and Mercy.

Pure love is the key that opens the door to God's home of Love and Mercy.

20
The Fantastic Spiritual Quest of Milarepa

*H*ow great is your devotion to find God?

Few can boast of the love, humility, and devotion of Milarepa, the eleventh-century saint and poet of the Tibetans. Oddly enough, he started out as a black magician.

In those long-ago days, other key events were playing out that would have a profound impact upon the future of mankind. Among them was the Vikings' discovery of North America. Then, too, the Chinese people perfected gunpowder, which would prove a devastating blow to all civilization.

It was also the time of the First Crusade. Some would argue that it opened a centuries-long religious war between the Christians and Muslims that lingers still to the present day.

And not to be forgotten was the birth of the spiritual giant Milarepa.

He was born into a wealthy family. At his father's early death, the young man seemed destined to a continued life of ease. But such was not to be the case.

Few can boast of the love, humility, and devotion of Milarepa. Oddly enough, he started out as a black magician.

Greedy relatives, whom Milarepa's father had entrusted with Milarepa's inheritance, stole it by devious means. They also reduced Milarepa's family to poverty. Embittered, his mother sent him in search of a black magician. She wished Milarepa to learn how to destroy them. So the youth set out to fulfill that mission.

He did find such a teacher and soon became practiced in the black arts and killed many of those relatives. They'd gathered for a wedding, and Milarepa caused the wedding house to collapse on their heads. But some survived.

Milarepa's next act of destruction then followed.

The barley crop that year was one of the most bountiful seen in many seasons. All the area's farmers, including his corrupt relatives, were rubbing their hands in glee, foreseeing granaries that would soon bulge with abundance.

But it was not to be.

Milarepa set out with his black arts and began to work spells. A terrific storm arose. Wind and hail beat the barley flat to the soil. This act is likely to have ruined the wealth of his relatives and perhaps even led to the starvation of some.

The frightened people determined to kill him. And so, young Milarepa was forced to flee for his life.

He sought out his teacher, who had bad news for him. Milarepa, he said, had made so much black karma that he'd better seek out a master of Buddhism and try to redeem some of that karma. It would ensure him of an easier incarnation the next time around.

A false start later, the ECK (Holy Spirit) finally led him to Marpa, the Translator, who was secretly also an ECK Master.

Marpa wasted no time at all in getting the reversal of Milarepa's karma under way.

This man was a no-nonsense and down-to-earth Master, who that day set out with two oxen to plow a field by the road. He brought some extra beer. His startled family noted that he had never plowed the fields before.

So why today?

In a short while, Milarepa came along the road, inquiring after Marpa, the great Yogi. Sharing the beer, Marpa promised Milarepa that he'd introduce him if he'd finish plowing the field.

So Milarepa plowed, and Marpa went home.

At day's end, a boy came to take Milarepa to Marpa's house. Marpa's wife had dreamed of Milarepa's arrival, but she didn't at all understand the spiritual tests that her husband had designed for him. So she interfered. That kept Milarepa from achieving the full purification that would have erased all his black karma. Twice she would intervene on Milarepa's behalf; twice it didn't sway Marpa at all.

Marpa first sketched out in the dirt a circular house of rocks. "Finish that," he said, "and I'll start you on the secret teachings."

But when the house was done, Marpa was greatly upset. "If I told you to build that," he said, "I must have drunk too much beer. Tear it down. Replace all the stones where you found them." Crushed, Milarepa did as he was told.

Marpa next told him to build a triangular house. "It'll be more suitable for my purposes," he said. Milarepa then asked Marpa's wife to be a witness to those instructions. Milarepa so hungered for the teachings that he set to it with a renewed heart. Partway through its construction, Marpa stormed up.

Marpa wasted no time at all in getting the reversal of Milarepa's karma under way.

"Who told you to build that?" he demanded.

"You did," said the youth. Marpa's wife took his side, but Marpa ignored her testimony.

"It must have been due to your sorcerer's tricks. Tear it down. Build me a square one of nine stories."

Milarepa again appealed to Marpa's wife to testify to those instructions, which she gladly did. She had no idea that she was interfering in a spiritual test.

Each, alone, must account for his own spiritual debts. No one else can do it for him.

The square tower involved untold hardships. They bruised and battered Milarepa in body, mind, and spirit, yet his devotion never once wavered. Marpa secretly noted his love for the secret teachings.

When the tower was finished, he called Milarepa and his wife to come before him.

"Had you not interfered," he rebuked his shame-faced wife, "he would have worked off all the karma from his practice of black magic. As it stands, a portion remains, which he must work out."

Her interference had led Milarepa on in his mistaken belief that another could intervene in his obligations before the exacting Law of Karma.

Now the question is this: Do you have the same patience and devotion that Milarepa once did?

"But I will give him the initiation that will allow him to begin receiving the secret teachings," said Marpa.

And so it was at long last and after many trials that Milarepa could study the ancient ECK teachings.

Now the question is this: Do you have the same patience and devotion that Milarepa once did?

And further, will your own love for truth carry you even to the heights of God-Realization itself?

21
The Nightingale's Song

*O*nce upon a time, in ancient China, there lived an emperor in a splendid palace. Have you heard his story? It contains an important lesson for you.

The emperor enjoyed the most luxurious splendor. The richest, most elegant robes were his dress; the royal rooms showed the most ornate lamps and decorations; and the food on his table was thought fit for heaven. He was a happy and satisfied man.

Many travelers came to the palace to enjoy his hospitality. And so also came the emperor of Japan, who drank in the countless things of beauty and saw and smelled the royal gardens. Once, he and his companions even ventured into the forest and beyond, to the sea. There, one quiet evening, they chanced upon the heart-lifting song of a nightingale.

So lovely was this plain brown bird's song that it haunted the emperor of Japan all the way back home to his own kingdom.

One day he sent a letter to the Chinese emperor. He thanked him for all his gracious hospitality and extended an invitation to visit Japan. But the part of the letter that caught the Chinese emperor's eye

So lovely was this plain brown bird's song that it haunted the emperor of Japan all the way back home to his own kingdom.

115

was a puzzling mention of a most beautiful and heavenly song by the nightingale. The Chinese emperor knew of no such bird.

"What's a nightingale?" he asked his courtiers.

No one knew.

"Well, find out!" said their lord.

So they made wide inquiries in the court but could locate not a single notable personage who'd ever heard a nightingale's song, let alone knew what sort of creature it was.

By luck, a lowly servant girl in the kitchen overheard other servants tell of the emperor's quest. None of them had been beyond the pavilions in the emperor's gardens either, and certainly not ever into the forest and the sea beyond. They were as mystified as the emperor and all his courtiers.

"But I often hear the nightingale's lovely song," the servant girl said. "I carry soup to my sick mother, who lives by the sea, every evening."

Word of her story filtered up in short order through the palace grapevine, where it came to the ears of the chief adviser to the emperor. He questioned the girl. Satisfied by the authenticity of her story, he and a party from the royal court determined to find the magical bird and listen to its melodies themselves. Would its songs be fit for their lord?

So the girl led them, that evening, to find the little nightingale. She led them past the gardens, into the forest beyond, and to the shores of the distant sea.

Yes, this was a sound worthy of the emperor.

There, at eventide, they saw the plain songbird and listened to its warbling melodies with mouths agape.

Yes, this was a sound worthy of the emperor.

The nightingale agreed to their request to return to the palace and sing for him. Yet with reluctance, it left its perch among the magnolia blossoms and came to court.

A golden perch was awaiting it. It took its place before the emperor and began to sing. The beauty of its song was such that it brought tears of joy to the emperor's eyes. And so, the nightingale sang many precious melodies for him that evening. When the hour grew late, he asked, "What reward can I offer you for your celestial songs?"

"Oh, none at all," said the nightingale. "Your tears are return enough."

And so it was that the nightingale became the most talked-about addition to the royal court. But the royal life held none of the serenity of the forest or the sea for the little bird. It wished to return there to its home. However, courtiers had tied silken threads to its legs so it could never fly away. They followed its every move.

Then one day its freedom came in a most unlikely guise. The emperor of Japan had sent the Chinese ruler a toy nightingale. Wind it up, and it sings again and again.

But it had no heart.

The emperor and his court were enchanted by the toy. They forgot about the real nightingale. Freed of its fetters, it flew home to its perch among the magnolia blossoms by the sea. The fishermen who worked on their nets were happy at its return. The emperor at first missed its joyful songs, but his courtiers told of the toy nightingale's advantages. It would sing whenever the emperor wished. It was never too tired. It needn't wait till evening to deliver its gift to needful ears.

One day its freedom came in a most unlikely guise.

But one day the toy broke. Its voice fell still. The emperor's health broke soon after, and the court imagined that his final days were near.

However, the nightingale by the sea caught wind of the emperor's illness. One evening, soon after, it appeared on the windowsill of the royal bedchamber and began to sing its healing melodies. The emperor awoke. With great joy he turned to his little friend and said, "Thank you for coming. I've missed you. Please stay with me here in the palace as in times past and let your songs fill these heartless halls."

But the nightingale replied, "The palace is not my home. My heart needs to restore its songs in the gardens, meadows, and forests by the sea."

"Then what made you come back this evening?" asked the emperor.

"I heard of your illness and remembered your tears of joy at my songs, so I came."

Indeed, the cold palace could not renew the nightingale's songs, but the nightingale promised to return often to sing for the emperor, to tell of fishermen by the sea, of frogs' gossip in ponds, of cows in the meadows, and of people going about their daily lives.

"I shall come often," said the nightingale, "but tell no one that I give you news from beyond the royal gates."

The emperor gave his word, and so their friendship endured for many long and happy years.

* * *

The moral of the story is to count your blessings. Open your eyes to the miracles around you: your friends, your good fortunes, for all that life has seen fit to send your way. Today comes but once. Recog-

Open your eyes to the miracles around you: your friends, your good fortunes, for all that life has seen fit to send your way.

nize its goodness. Open your heart. Listen to a bird's trill and your sweetheart's whispers, feel the warmth of a dear one's kiss.

All is of the holy ECK, the Spirit of Life.

And remember the nightingale.

 ## Spiritual Exercise: Mahanta, I Love You

This spiritual exercise can be done while falling asleep, silently chanting HU or your personal word.

Start with a simple postulate, something very open and easy such as, "Mahanta, I love you." Then quietly, in the background of the mind, begin to sing HU. Just let it run on spiritual automatic. But automatic doesn't mean letting it turn into a meaningless mental repetition. Rather, in a very real sense, you remain conscious that the HU is rolling within you.

If you wake up in the middle of the night, you can spiritualize your consciousness by briefly putting your attention on the Mahanta, even for a second or two.

Know that you do this because you love God. You love the divine part within yourself. In this gentle, unpushy way, you become the lover of all life.

In this gentle, unpushy way, you become the lover of all life.

It's so easy to stay on track. Follow the Mahanta, the Living ECK Master. He'll guide you through all the fears and illusions that accompany change.

CHAPTER FIVE

Facing Hardships

22

When One
Door Closes . . .

*L*ong before a truth seeker finds the teachings of Eckankar, the invisible hand of the ECK, Divine Spirit, can be traced in his spiritual guidance.

Alexander Graham Bell, the inventor, said, "When one door closes another door opens; but we often look so long and so regretfully upon the closed door, that we do not see the ones which open for us."

And so also for me.

The wisdom, guidance, and protection of the ECK was a steady companion from my youth on. To be sure, Its presence went unnoticed. Do we question the abundance of the air we breathe or the water we drink?

Life offers all the exact measure of experience needed for spiritual growth.

My high-school days, at face value, looked like a string of misfortunes—at least that's the way I regarded them for a long time. However, after I learned about Eckankar and the guidance of the ECK Masters, the pieces fell into place.

The wisdom, guidance, and protection of the ECK was a steady companion from my youth on. To be sure, Its presence went unnoticed.

The boarding school I went to was noted for its top-notch education. Yet it was also a narrow, stifling atmosphere. It could have quenched the fire of my spiritual inquiry, for I loved and feared God. Odd circumstances took place, which the following snapshot of my four years in high school shows to a small degree.

Where the rigid religious system became a threat to my spiritual development, a door opened to let in fresh air for Soul.

But where the rigid religious system became a threat to my spiritual development, a door opened to let in fresh air for Soul.

Please read the events that follow from the high viewpoint of Soul. In that light, my failure in scholastics also paved the way for my independent development and inquiry.

*   *   *

My searching nature could have been shut down at any time in my youth, but it remained open. Thanks to silent help from the ECK and the ECK Masters.

By age thirteen, I made the decision to accompany my buddy and cousin, Jerry, to preministerial school in Milwaukee. The decision caused a family upheaval. But I was smitten of God. Never mind the school's beautiful swimming pool.

Freshman. Six roommates: three sophomores, three of us lowly freshmen. A rigid hierarchy meant things like riding the floor buffer while a sophomore operated it. My weight on the machine would enhance the floor's sheen, or so ran a theory.

And two hours of mandatory study each school night. A quiet period enforced by the dorm floor's two college proctors. Nightly torture.

But there was lots of food at the school's family-style dining hall. A sophomore roommate at my table enjoyed a big appetite. Mine matched his, a source of wonder and appreciation on his part. Bill's connections at neighboring tables allowed us to scrounge their uneaten mashed potatoes, meat, and dessert. Thanks to Bill and the invisible hand of ECK, the food was an antidote for a runaway case of homesickness. Yet soon, my once-excellent eyesight began to suffer from an overload of sweet foods and snacks.

Classroom seats, assigned by alphabet, put me in the very last row of *A* division. The professor's chalk marks on the board were like spiderwebs. Algebraic equations and the like—mere scribblings in the distance. Grades dove.

Sophomore. The foundation of future studies had cracked beyond repair in a year's time, but I held on. I was a marginal student and grew used to it.

Also, in this second year at boarding school, severe migraine headaches added to the problem of poor eyesight. Both ensured my status as a hanging-on-by-the-teeth student.

Cause of the migraines?

Our dorm, built some fifty years earlier, got its first face-lift the summer between my freshman and sophomore years. Lead paint was slathered on the walls. It covered decades of grime. The smell of the lead paint caused terrible headaches, so that I spent many days after class flat on the bunk bed.

Junior. A new dorm. More freedom, less oversight by an in-your-face college proctor. My five roommates, *A* and *B* students, were a studious and religious bunch. They undertook my spiritual disciplines. One or the other of them tried to escort me to the mandatory, twice-a-day chapel services.

Thanks to Bill and the invisible hand of ECK, the food was an antidote for a runaway case of homesickness.

I liked chapel, in general. But I chafed at having guards.

Soon my circle of friends widened to include classmates versed in the art of skipping chapel with a minimum of risk. The intrigue of sidestepping chapel checks by dorm proctors proved a real challenge. It was my rebellion against rigid rules.

That year also, an observant professor told me to get a pair of glasses. It was a humbling moment. I'd been proud of good eyesight. But glasses brought new life and color to my surroundings.

The migraines, in the meantime, quit too.

Senior. My roommate was a would-be disc jockey for a radio station. Don, even more misplaced than I, loved loud, blaring rock-and-roll music. The noise drove me from our study room, a good reason to let my studies slide again.

But I was not a stupid lad. When my Latin grade crashed to a *D*, my parents were forced to pay for a tutor. That stung my sense of pride and responsibility.

My Latin teacher showed me how to build a foundation for learning. The ECK was helping me through his tutelage.

The tutor was Professor Anderson, my Latin teacher. He set me to learn the seven irregular verbs in all their tenses and voices. I came to love them. In that way, Anderson showed me how to build a foundation for learning. The ECK was helping me through his tutelage.

To our mutual satisfaction, my Latin grade soared to a *B* by year's end. It was a stunning comeback and a proud achievement.

The senior year was a turning point in my self-discipline. Poor study habits would still haunt the college years to come; nevertheless there was hope. I now began to study on my own. In time, the missing foundation of mathematics and literature began to fill in.

*   *   *

Why put you to such a history of apparent failure as a student? It was not all downhill.

There *were* some classes I came to love: religion, German, New Testament Greek, Latin, and literature (but not English grammar, please). Into those classes, I put my heart. They were necessary for my life's mission as the Mahanta, the Living ECK Master.

Each failure or poor grade looked like a closing door. Yet each class I gave my heart to opened the door to new self-respect.

Early on, I had low self-esteem because of low grades. But in time I learned how all the distractions over the years had kept me from embracing the rigid, dead forms of an orthodox religion. I wanted, indeed craved, the living truth.

In the end, I came to find and appreciate the ECK teachings. Divine Spirit had lent silent but sure guidance all along the way.

Divine Spirit had lent silent but sure guidance all along the way.

23
Change Is, Oh, So Hard

*This thing called change affects us on both a personal and social level. As individuals, we find it's smart to conform to the standards of those in our immediate community or else suffer for it in some way.

Look, for example, at one who's been a lifelong member of a church and one day decides he must go elsewhere for his spiritual unfoldment. Living within the anonymity of a municipality makes one's change of belief easier because few of the other church members are likely to know him on a personal level. There'd only be his family to resolve a change with—still an unpleasant undertaking.

But it'd be different in a rural community, or in a small town where there's only one church, one religion, and everybody knows everybody. In a close blending like that of the personal and social areas, change to a new religion would pose more misunderstandings. Even censure.

So where is this going?

As an ECKist, you are a member of a "new" spiritual teaching under the name of Eckankar. Let's say you've been an ECKist a year or two. Most

Look, for example, at one who's been a lifelong member of a church and one day decides he must go elsewhere for his spiritual unfoldment.

129

of the personal and immediate tumult lies in the past. It's done. That heavy karma is finished.

The longer you're in Eckankar, the more likely it is that you'll move into some capacity of leadership. A Vahana, an ECK missionary, is especially aware of the subtle tides of thoughts and emotions that flow in the community.

Introduce a new element, like the ECK teachings, into a place, and you can be assured of a reaction—either mild or strong.

Let's just say here that the more things change, the more they stay the same.

Bringing the ECK teachings into our personal and social world can be a trial or an enrichment for all. It's in the doing.

Now, bringing the ECK teachings into our personal and social world can likewise be a trial or an enrichment for all. It's in the doing.

Here again we face the conflict between love and power. There will be more harmony if a Vahana remembers to respect the just values of the community and is not heedless of others' feelings. In short, it's all about love, consideration, and all that the two entail.

History is a fair teacher. Let's take a look, then, at the persecutions that took place in England when its society said good-bye to the church of Rome, the Catholic Church.

It was the Middle Ages. The Reformation had swept the continent of Europe. Finally, it came to England.

But the lower class liked and needed the festivals of the Catholic Church, like the many fairs it sponsored to raise money to feed and clothe the poor. These fairs provided the lower-class youth a chance to meet, make sport, and thus marry and raise their own families.

Then came the Calvinistic teachings of the

Reformation. It attempted to change the whole social order. The Puritans and the Presbyterians followed a teaching that allowed for no fun.

No more all-day Sunday fairs.

Instead, their plan of salvation had a severe face and body to it. Everybody could go to church for a couple of hours in the morning. Then, at home, the father was to discuss the sermon with his family in detail. That evening, for fun, they could return to church for yet another service.

You can see how wrong this teaching was for the lower class. How would the young meet, have a good time, and find suitable mates? Guess the outcome. As could be expected, society wanted no part of the Calvinistic teachings in that form. They posed a threat to the social order.

One might have predicted the severe persecutions that fell upon the Puritans and Presbyterians.

In a more recent case, a Missouri Synod Lutheran pastor tried several times to change the doctrinal rigor of his church. (This was the synod of my pre-ECK church.)

After the September 11, 2001, tragedy at the World Trade Center in New York, this pastor joined in an ecumenical prayer session with clerics of other faiths. The assembly included Muslims, Jews, Sikhs, and Hindus. Among the Christians were Baptists, Roman Catholics, and others. But that denomination of the Lutheran Church has a rule against such intermingling with other faiths.

The pastor had committed a big error, the second of its kind.

On the face of it, his church might well be deemed wrong to censure him. But a review of church history shows why the Lutheran Church—Missouri

This pastor joined in an ecumenical prayer session with clerics of other faiths. The assembly included Muslims, Jews, Sikhs, and Hindus.

Synod had made the strict rule about its pastors not joining in the prayer services of other faiths.

In the early nineteenth century, the king of Prussia told Lutherans to worship with Calvinists. That'd be as if a political leader, like, say, the president of the United States, issued an edict that ECKists were to worship with Lutherans, Catholics, or Presbyterians. It wouldn't fly.

In protest, then, Lutherans fled from Prussia to Australia and the United States, where some settled in New York and Missouri. Hence, a Missouri-Synod Lutheran Church.

What's all that to do with us?

Change is relentless. It picks upon the just and the unjust alike. It occurs outside of Eckankar when we come into contact with other people. Even more to the point, change also causes consternation within Eckankar.

For example, the not-too-distant future will see factions arise—say, the "Paulists." These will insist upon some minor point that they've fixed upon from the time of Paul Twitchell, the first spiritual leader of the present incarnation of the ECK teachings. They'll be rigid in thought. Unable or unwilling to grow with the outer trappings needed to conform to the basic requirements of society, they will rebel against change.

The Living ECK Master of the times is the Living Word.

These rebels will fix on the outer form of Paul Twitchell instead of recognizing the rocklike foundation of the ECK teachings that the Living ECK Master of the times is the Living Word. His mission is to find and then lift people into higher states beyond the human consciousness.

It's so easy to stay on track. Follow the Mahanta, the Living ECK Master. He'll guide you through all fears and illusions that accompany change.

Yes, for some, change is, oh, so hard. But for one who loves Sugmad (God) it is a rich, fulfilling opportunity.

24
When Worlds Collide or Burn

*I*n part, this title is like that of an old movie. When Earth is on a collision course with an object from space, worldwide pandemonium takes place.

The unknown is a threat to the known.

People panic. They lose their heads. But in the end all works out and the human race survives, although in a new context and with a change in consciousness.

The living heave a global sigh of relief as the threat leaves them. What next?

That is the same response a seeker of truth faces on the path to God. The seeker lives a well-ordered life. The todays are like most yesterdays, and the expectation is for the tomorrows to mirror the good things of today.

Then the seeker meets a hard object that hurtles into his routine. The building blocks of his well-patterned world burst into pieces.

The old comfortable things rock. Fear clutches the heart.

In the end all works out and the human race survives, although in a new context and with a change in consciousness.

Where is the Master?

Some time ago an ECKist we'll call Lois came into a tunnel of sadness. She awoke each day feeling like an ant stuck in a pool of molasses, finding every effort a taxing exercise. (She'd quit eating sugar months ago. It used to cause lethargy and a general tiredness.)

So Lois made some changes.

She began to alter routines. She tried experiments like doing the spiritual exercises upon awakening rather than before leaving for work. No improvement.

Next, she tried different holy words during contemplation. But sadness kept its tight hold.

Lois then asked the Mahanta, the Inner Master, "What's wrong with me?"

He gave her a nudge how to find guidance. It was to open *The Shariyat-Ki-Sugmad* (The Way of the Eternal) at random before going to sleep. It gave a clue of how to proceed. Here's what she read:

> He is mainly concerned with being himself and living, which means that he has learned to live with himself through self-discipline. He is responsible to himself and works toward a happiness which becomes a part of the whole of himself. In other words, he is integrated and is now a part of the universe instead of being only a part of his community, nation, and race.

That was the clue.

In the night Lois had an unsettling dream that showed her living a halfhearted life.

In the night Lois had an unsettling dream that gave a bigger picture of the state she was in.

It showed her living a halfhearted life. Further, it warned that her dearest love was at risk of being lost. The thought of such a loss tore at her heart. She cried at the dream's warning.

However upon awakening Lois felt none of the devastation upon her emotions that one would expect. The dream left her buoyant and cheerful. She felt better than she had in weeks—loved—and she couldn't wait to get started on the day.

The dream showed how she'd shut herself off from life. Her dream was a shock treatment. It catapulted her right out of the tunnel of sadness.

The Mahanta had shown her a worst-case scenario. It got her full attention. Life was sweet.

At bedtime the next evening Lois opened *The Shariyat* again. It said:

> He soon learns in this struggle between the ego and his true self, Soul, that nothing he can do is right, spontaneous, or genuine; he cannot act independently of himself. On all sides is nothing but defeat. But in this moment of defeat, he, the agent of all his actions, cannot act, does not act, and does not see any future, past, or present in his life which is worthy of anything.
>
> When he has come to this point the realization bursts upon him that he has nothing to prove and nothing to lose; he has only to be himself and live independent of all other things.

As Lois read this passage, tears of joy and understanding blurred her eyes.

The Mahanta, the Living ECK Master works in wondrous ways. As the Outer Master, he'd provided the printed ECK bible that gave Lois the first clue to the wall of sadness that stood as an obstacle in her spiritual path. Then, as the Inner Master, he'd given her a wake-up dream.

The Mahanta, the Living ECK Master works in wondrous ways. As the Inner Master, he'd given her a wake-up dream.

*   *   *

When the Light and Sound of God strike the consciousness of someone in a rut, the aftermath is like the collision of two worlds. The immediate effect is chaos.

Yet changes through that Word of God bring changes of a positive order. Old thoughts and habits burst apart. But the Word of God, the ECK, working through the dual activity of Light and Sound, replaces stagnation and fear with the rejuvenating power of divine love.

In a sense, a chela (spiritual student) from Ghana saw his world in crisis too. Let's call him Joseph.

He reported a strong spiritual experience. Yet it was more like a burning of his world than a collision.

In a dream the Mahanta met him and all the active members of ECK in his family: parents and siblings. The Master gave instructions to the group. The family asked for and received his spiritual advice as well as new techniques for their use.

Finally, the Mahanta led them in a HU Chant.

The HU chant is a love song to God. It comes from the heart of God, and the ECK Masters have taught it to mankind from early history on.

This chant is a love song to God. It comes from the heart of God, and the ECK Masters have taught it to mankind from early history on. It survived in several tribal traditions in this age, before the ECK teachings exploded into modern society in 1965 through the efforts of Paul Twitchell.

In Joseph's dream, he felt an unbearable heat rising from the holy word, HU. He calls this a "baptism of fire."

Joseph ran from the Master, who continued to sing HU. The Master kept apace.

The heat was such that the sky caught fire. In a panic Joseph ran faster, but to no avail. The Master was tight on his heels. This experience was like the burning of Sodom and Gomorrah in the Old Testament and the tongues like fire on Pentecost—both rolled into one.

In a nutshell, this holy fire of ECK burned away old karma in Joseph. It was an instrument of spiritual purification. Heavy loads were gone. After that, Joseph felt the joy and lightness of a greater degree of freedom.

When worlds collide or burn: in ECK, it means a renewal.

25

You, the Master, and Change

*W*hat, more changes?" some of you ask. "Why can't things stay the same as they used to be?"

Frankly, nothing is ever the same as it used to be. The ECK (Divine Spirit) is again bringing some necessary changes to the way we do things in Eckankar. In Its all-encompassing wisdom, It is adjusting old things. The Mahanta, the Living ECK Master will in the future make only several appearances a year at ECK seminars instead of the many that everyone is used to. Some of these appearances will be by live satellite link. The ECK makes his health the reason.

Change often upsets people. As bad as conditions might be, at least they represent a known factor and give people a sense of comfort and stability. Change, however, rocks the boat.

Yet understanding the nature of change is an important part of your spiritual life. Note these words from *The Shariyat-Ki-Sugmad* (the holy scriptures of ECK):

Understanding the nature of change is an important part of your spiritual life.

141

The matter world is but an extension of consciousness with a crust of solidity that must be broken. All the illusions of the Kal are but a part of material creation. This is fluid and bends to the creativeness of Soul. Those who retreat from life and do nothing are as bound in matter as are those who believe in the concept of a solid universe. Body and spirit are not separated from life but are a part of it as much as Soul. The nature of this world is change and impermanence (Book One, p. 151).

It says elsewhere that there is and always will be change in how things appear. In human terms it is called "birth and growth, evolution and progress, age and death."

The Mahanta, the Living ECK Master's mission is solely to help each Soul find the most direct way home to God.

Reform Is Not the Goal

The Mahanta, the Living ECK Master does not appear on earth to bring about social, economic, or political reforms. His mission is solely to help each Soul find the most direct way home to God.

However, he does point out to his followers the spiritual pitfalls that surround them in their daily lives.

He clearly points out the five passions of the mind. These five include lust, greed, anger, vanity, and an undue attachment to material things. Once he points to examples of a particular passion, or vice, as it makes an appearance in the follower's own life, however, there is often an emotional reaction on the part of the ECKist. The ECKist becomes angry.

"Why doesn't the Living ECK Master keep his nose out of politics?"

The chela (spiritual student) does not want to understand that the Master may actually have been talking about the spiritual dangers of greed. That is the vice of wanting to have the property of someone else without paying for it in the true coin. This vice is linked to theft. People try (successfully) to steal the property of others through the courts by filing lawsuits to gain a huge return for themselves. Or it may be an economic system that takes the property of people and redistributes it to others. It's still greed.

Who respects the old commandment today, "Thou shalt not steal"?

None of these five passions stands alone, however. Since they are all a part of the human condition, we see that other passions give support to a primary passion that is part of the karmic makeup of an individual. So vanity may, for example, support the outer signs of greed.

In this case, the greedy one desires the necklace, the savings, or maybe the spouse of another. Vanity whispers in his ear, "It's OK. You deserve it!" One vice supports another.

It is these passions and their manifestations in daily life that the Mahanta, the Living ECK Master warns his followers to be on the lookout for. These are spiritual pitfalls. If the wheel of karma's hold on people is ever to let go, then some sort of change must take place in their states of consciousness.

But those five passions of the mind are like favorite pets. "Keep your hands off my doggie!"

The ECK Brings Change

So even though neither the Living ECK Master nor his true followers try to make reforms in the social, economic, or political structure of the society in which they live, far-reaching changes do occur

It is these passions and their manifestations in daily life that the Mahanta, the Living ECK Master warns his followers to be on the lookout for.

anyway. But it's not because the Master is an activist. He is not. However, the ECK (the Holy Spirit) does sometimes cause upheavals wherever he goes. It happens simply because he is a clear channel for the divine power, which brings about any and all changes of Its own volition.

Who can stand in the way of Spirit?

Initiates at each level are affected by change in a somewhat different manner.

A Second Initiate stands at a crossroads with three roads to choose from. He will in time learn that his perfection depends upon taking not the high or low roads, but the middle road. Then he also becomes a channel for the ECK.

At the Third Initiation, one learns that these three roads are actually forces: the positive, the negative, and the neutral. He notices that all change is a direct result of these three forces working upon each other, and that all are under the control of Kal, the Satan or negative power. Yet these forces help Soul reach perfection.

A Fifth Initiate learns more about change and how one must allow the ECK into his consciousness at home, work, or play. It will then bring him to a higher state of awareness. Yet the Kal is a real problem. It tries to create doubt about the teachings of ECK in the Mahdis' mind and pull him back into the lower worlds. And sometimes it succeeds.

So always sing your personal, holy word of love to God for strength, wisdom, and understanding.

Yes, there will be changes in Eckankar. It's the ECK shaking the Tree of Life again to see who will stay and who will go. It's ever the same old cycle.

It's the Wind of Change.

26
God Waits for You
within the Problem

A woman had a problem. Her children had grown and left the nest. Full of love, she now wanted to serve people and ECK (the Holy Spirit) by giving talks and workshops on the teachings of ECK.

But only members of Eckankar came to her workshop. No one else.

She is also the Arahata (teacher) for a book discussion class on *Stranger by the River* by Paul Twitchell. While preparing a lesson, the Mahanta (Inner Master) spoke to her through the secret, inner lines of communication. It's like a private phone line.

"God waits for you within the problem," he said.

This response took her by surprise.

Yet in reviewing the way she had treated problems her whole life, she had an insight. An image from the movie *The Guns of Navarone* came to mind. The movie ends with the scene of two huge artillery pieces embedded near the top of a steep cliff. The weapons turn slowly to focus their aim.

The Mahanta (Inner Master) spoke to her through the secret, inner lines of communication.

Immediately, she realized she was the cliff and the guns.

All this lifetime she'd tried to blow apart and destroy problems with self-help, creative visualizations, and anything else that promised to rid her of them. She felt it necessary to destroy problems in order to continue her journey home to God.

Then, the Mahanta's whisper taught her better. "God waits for you within the problem," he'd whispered.

She's learned to examine all parts of a problem with love, because a spiritual lesson lies at its heart.

Now she knows that getting rid of problems is not the answer. Instead, she's learned to examine all parts of a problem with love, because a spiritual lesson lies at its heart. Every problem is a teacher.

Once, I too had a similar problem. The Mahanta also told me how to approach it, and the solution is still an integral part of my way of teaching ECK today. That's how I learned to tell stories.

* * *

Many years ago as an initiate of Paul Twitchell, the Mahanta, the Living ECK Master then, I ran into a problem when telling new people about the ECK teachings. Actually, it was two problems.

First, new people did come to the ECK introductory talks that I helped present, but as an audience their interest in the whole ECK presentation often flagged quickly. Second, my part of the presentation met with criticism from a few ECKists. Something could work better.

So I asked Paul in contemplation for the answer.

"How can I give a talk that appeals to an audience but still avoids the unjustified criticism of some ECKists about my understanding of ECK doctrines?" I asked.

Paul said cryptically, "Look to your past." Soon thereafter he opened my understanding some more.

"You won't please people all the time," he said. "So overlook the undue criticism." (Indeed, some of their suggestions were well-taken.)

Yet his instruction, "Look to your past," was much harder to decipher. Look for what? In time, he again opened my Spiritual Eye to see the answer. What form of communication between people had held the greatest interest for me?

In time, Paul again opened my Spiritual Eye to see the answer. Tell stories. People like them.

Mainly, public communication was by talking or writing. They were lower forms of the Sound and Light of God in expression, to use for good or ill.

Looking far back to my childhood, I remembered the many stories Mother and her two sisters told in the kitchen while baking and cooking for meals. Their light talk about the doings of neighbors and relatives was delightful. In short, they told stories. But whenever the stories became too interesting for young ears, Mother shooed me out of the kitchen.

That is only one of many examples from my past, and no doubt, you could supply plenty of your own. Telling stories is a powerful way to communicate.

Storytelling also applies to the written word. Later, in some other ECK writings, I may tell more of my introduction to stories and the important role they played in shaping my future life.

Here, an examination of my past had provided the answer to my question of Paul. Tell stories. People like them.

In looking around since then, I came to realize the impact of storytelling among people, regardless of time or culture. Look around. How many million people go to the movies each week? Movies are stories. How many more times do they turn on the TV to catch their favorite situation comedy, movie, or soap opera?

People are always telling each other stories. Parents relate the funny things a child has done. Grandparents are notorious for that. Even people's complaints are stories.

A story has three parts: a beginning, a middle, and an end. Otherwise it isn't a story.

What's a good story? One that has a good beginning, a good middle, and a good end. And an excellent story? Well, it has an excellent beginning, an excellent middle, and an excellent end. Use the latter for ECK talks.

So to give a public ECK talk or even a workshop, be sure that its foundation is stories. Then hitch the ECK doctrines to them in an equal proportion.

If some members of the audience later want a fuller explanation about an ECK doctrine, you'll see how the storytelling format has opened their hearts.

Storytelling is the honey, and the ECK doctrines are the bread. They go well together.

* * *

An ECKist learned what a joy life can be when one lets the Holy Spirit steer it.

That was an important lesson for me.

An ECKist, in the following dream, learned what a joy life can be when one lets the Holy Spirit steer it.

She was a passenger in a car. Wah Z, today's Mahanta, the Living ECK Master, stood outside her open door on a running board. The car took corners, went up and down hills—but without a driver at the wheel. Yet the car reacted perfectly to road conditions. Wah Z looked directly into her eyes.

"Do you *see* anyone applying the brakes?" he asked.

To her, it meant Life had taken over, because ECK is the force between the road and car. So there is a perfect balance of road (impersonal, divine love) and car (her free will). It was a realization that life's problems would not be a problem so long as she was a conscious passenger to the will of ECK.

She only had to open her heart and ears to the Mahanta.

So, do the Spiritual Exercises of ECK. They'll help keep your private phone line open to the Mahanta.

The Spiritual Exercises of ECK help keep your private phone line open to the Mahanta.

27
The Dark Night of Soul

*T*he dark nights of Soul come in all flavors and sizes. All the flavors are too bitter; all the sizes, too large. Not at all like an ice-cream cone or melt-in-your-mouth candy bar.

None of this is to belittle the bruising and downright awful pain that accompanies a dark night of Soul, whatever its dimensions. Its duration is always too long, like a worrisome illness that sits by the bedside with an overbearing presence which only the spears of sun's early light can drive to flight.

St. John of the Cross coined the phrase "dark night of the soul." It's the season an individual thinks God has forsaken him, and that he is left to his own devices on the battlefield of life.

Yet the Mahanta, the Lord of Hosts, stands by his side.

Why, then, does the Master not appear?

St. Gregory gave an answer when he said, "If without any doubt the darkness of ignorance is the night of the soul, the understanding is not improperly styled the day."

The day of understanding follows the night. Always and ever. No matter how long or dark the night may be.

The day of understanding follows the night. Always and ever.

A certain woman with many creative talents has suffered a fair number of the dark nights of Soul. The onslaughts on the physical end of the spectrum were, to her, the most shattering kind one could suffer. But time and healing put those fears to flight. The wheel of fortune has turned again, however. This time its pointer rests upon a place of arid sands of the least inviting kind.

Life has set her in a desert.

This trial is not of storm, as was the physical ordeal now passed. It is of the heart. Like the corrosion of acid upon hard steel, it robs the spirit of its will to endure, to await the golden light of understanding.

Like the day, understanding will always defeat the night of ignorance.

Patience.

Love and patience.

And let God's holy name of HU be always on your lips.

From where does the pain of ignorance get its sting, its ability to wound and make tears shed?

Aesop once told of a boy with the misfortune to brush a stinging nettle with his hand. Crying, he ran to his mother to kiss and make it better. "My dear son," she said when his tears had ceased, "the next time you're near a nettle plant, grasp it firmly. Then it'll feel as soft as silk." (Don't try this at home.)

Ignorance of stinging nettles had led him into a patch, but fear should not keep him away. Herbalists report many healing and nutritional benefits to the credit of nettles.

Fear keeps people from grasping a nettle plant. It's the very nature of timidity to do the wrong thing, so they avoid facing a fear. But this fear

Let God's holy name of HU be always on your lips.

returns. With a new face on the morrow, it deceives and beguiles the senses, feelings, and thoughts. And it's, again, a stranger with a mask. Yet the character behind the mask is the old foe ignorance. It is of the same stuff; indeed, it is the very twin of the misconception of truth that has come before.

What is the nature of this ignorance?

It is always of the same kind, until the individual has the courage to grasp the next nettle with a firm and confident hand.

So, too, an ECK initiate should ask, "What am I unwilling to face?"

You can be sure it's something. It's also likely that it'll be of the same species as the plant that has caused so much tribulation in the past. For example, many people let the *social consciousness* dictate their thoughts, feelings, and actions. "What will people think?" is the motivator instead of "What do I know in my heart of hearts is the right thing to do?"

A young mother has let the social consciousness play an ever-larger role in the direction of her life. One has not even to ask, and she's quick to point out her love and devotion to ECK.

Is she being honest with herself?

Well, does she find time for the Spiritual Exercises of ECK? Sometimes, in a haphazard way. But only if not too tired from running all day long to fulfill social obligations to her Christian family and friends. A question that begs an airing is, "So what does your child know about ECK and the Mahanta?" And again, "Is the child doing the spiritual exercises?"

Likely, the answer would be negative for the questions above. The social consciousness tugs at

So, too, an ECK initiate should ask, "What am I unwilling to face?"

the emotions. It leads a chela into the night.

The dark night of Soul hangs on like a turtle, unwilling to let go once it has a hold.

For example, a man lost a good salary when his job disappeared in a down business cycle. Like many, he'd bought a house, car, and other goods on credit. Time rolled on. His savings dwindled like sand in an hourglass, a steady trickle. He'd done all the right things. He mailed his résumé to companies in his line of work, asked friends to keep their eyes open, and remembered to include the Mahanta, the Living ECK Master as a counselor.

Nothing came of all his efforts.

His brave heart and mind began to wilt under the heart of growing financial woes. House, car, and goods went on the for-sale block. Even so, prospective buyers were slow to call. Nor were they willing to pay the asking price. It was a buyer's market.

All too soon his possessions were gone. He was scratching for money to cover the basic needs of food, shelter, and clothing.

A spiritual gift that came of his trial is the ability to read the true motives of others. The mask of social consciousness has slipped from his eyes.

What was his reaction to this dark night of Soul? After all, most of his treasures had fled.

Did he blame the Master?

Not on your life. He took full responsibility for his downfall. "What is it that I don't see?" he asked again and again. In the end he understood his blind spot: He needed to be liked too much—a crutch of the social consciousness.

Yet now, the Master appeared to have opened a new portal to spiritual unfoldment. Things are looking up, he says.

A spiritual gift that came of his trial is the ability to read the true motives of others. The mask of social consciousness has slipped from his eyes.

His dark night of Soul displaced his ignorance and in its place bestowed a firmer foundation for the temple of truth inside him.

 Spiritual Exercise: Game of Chess

You can do this exercise anytime—whether you are at work, in contemplation, or about to fall asleep.

Lightly place your attention upon a situation in your life, then put your viewpoint as Soul above the situation. Look down on everything going on below as if it were a chess game—even though it might be in your imagination. You can look at a situation anywhere in the world from this viewpoint.

As you are gazing upon it, change the situation by simply rearranging your place on the chessboard. It's a successful device, and those who use it often make great changes around themselves.

Lightly place your attention upon a situation in your life, then put your viewpoint as Soul above the situation.

God's love showed itself to her turtle friend through her act of kindness.

CHAPTER SIX

The Gift of Service

28
A Single Yellow Rose

*L*ove *does* make the world go around.

An ECK initiate generally came to work early. From her window she could see the other employees arrive for work, and also watch the day begin. It was autumn. Outside her window was a rosebush, going to sleep after the kisses of several frosts.

One morning, in early November, she noticed the bush was trying very hard to bloom once more. A stem appeared, then a single bud.

How could a rose expect to bloom so late in fall?

The little rosebud captured the attention of the ECKist as, day by day, it struggled to grow against impossible odds. She felt such love for the little bud. And as the little rosebud grew, so did her love for it.

At night she put a small plastic bag over the bud to protect it against the night's chill, to allow it to awaken to the sun's smile in the morning. Maybe it would bloom yet.

One morning, as she removed the plastic bag, the little rosebud seemed stressed. Did it want to come inside? Surely, the temperature had grown less friendly, and the rosebud's last chance to bloom

The little rosebud captured the attention of the ECKist as, day by day, it struggled to grow against impossible odds.

was fast slipping away. It wanted to come in.

So our friend snipped it free from the bush, took it inside, and carefully placed it in a vase. Then she added water.

That very day this little rosebud began to bloom. By nightfall it was nearly in full bloom, there beside a picture of the Master.

A single yellow rose.

The ECK initiate wondered about the meaning behind this single rosebud's mighty effort to spread forth, unfold, against all odds.

An incident early in the week then came to mind. An inmate at a correctional institution had sent a request over the Internet for information about Eckankar. She'd remembered him from a recent newscast and had felt compassion for him.

Retiring that evening, she reflected idly upon his name, one name among countless others in the news.

That night she had a Soul Travel experience under the Master's guidance. When the rapid movement had ceased, she became aware of herself in the prisoner's cell. He was surprised to see a visitor.

"Be easy," she said. "I come with the permission of the Living ECK Master."

Their conversation took many turns. She was aware of helping him understand some difficult issues. The Master next opened her eyes to look back in his life to boyhood. Some painful events had occurred then which set up conditions that played out later in life, leading finally to this jail cell.

When the Soul Travel experience ended, she reflected upon the lesson of the little rosebud.

It reminded her of all Souls everywhere touched by the Mahanta. They were searching for divine

It reminded her of all Souls everywhere touched by the Mahanta. They were searching for divine love.

love. Instinctively, they knew it would take them home again. But where to look?

"When the student is ready, the Master appears." Surely, it's the age-old story retold many thousands of times about the Master Gardener and each precious, single rosebud.

*   *   *

Life goes on with or without us.

A dear woman had lost her mate some time ago. Her heart was heavy. Alone in this world, missing his love and companionship, she often wondered how long she could endure the pain of separation and loneliness.

She was trying to let go and move on. Yet her wounded heart needed time to heal.

One night she did a Spiritual Exercise of ECK with the intention of letting go of the painful memories. Two healing dreams came to her.

In the first, she saw her mate. He was both healthy and very happy.

The second showed him again, as she'd known him in his final days on earth: full of cancer and very weak. But she noticed his attitude. In spite of all, he was completely happy and had total detachment about his illness. Both dreams confirmed what the Mahanta, the Living ECK Master had told her in a personal letter.

Now she knew of her mate's joy by her own experience.

Another dream of importance came some days later. She was in the inner court of a prison. Her mate was there, talking with a young couple. He waved when he saw her and signaled that he'd come by in a minute.

Surely, it's the age-old story retold many thousands of times about the Master Gardener and each precious, single rosebud.

Other miracles happened to this dear woman later in the day. She called it "a real day of liberation."

Freed from the prison of past remembrances, she faced yet another. Her way of communicating with the Inner Master, the Mahanta, was no longer working. She found herself in a prison of expectation.

It meant this: she was forever waiting for a confirmation of the Mahanta's love for her.

So she changed her attitude and searched for new ways. What she realized was that it's enough to give love to the Mahanta, to feel it in her heart, but without expectation of any kind. It's enough to simply give love and know that it's returned a thousandfold.

Since letting go of her pain, she's met another ECKist. This man with a beautiful heart has touched hers, like a sunbeam giving life, love, and comfort to a rosebud.

*   *   *

Soul, a rosebud, senses Its destiny: to reach God-Realization.

Soul, a rosebud, senses Its destiny: to reach God-Realization. It's the state of total love, true love. It touches the Almighty and yet reaches down to the lowest in creation.

*   *   *

Another ECKist, preparing a workshop on my book *A Modern Prophet Answers Your Key Questions about Life*, came across a statement. It was to this effect: "You do not have to Soul Travel to be successful in ECK. Another way to God-Realization is to give tender love and care to every action, because of your love for God."

The idea left her in awe. "Oh, I can do that!" she said.

A month earlier, a spiritual exercise had brought her to a beautiful forest in the heavenly worlds. The Master walked with her. They came to a bench and sat to rest.

There it dawned on her: "Oh, I can have God-Realization too—even as a woman!"

Until then, she didn't realize she had harbored such a limiting attitude. Not until it was gone did she note its longtime hold on her.

So many Soulbuds are looking for the truth of ages. The sunbeams of divine love dance upon their prisons, and the fullness of time will yet see a garden full of yellow roses. You and many others.

But a single yellow rose at a time.

The fullness of time will yet see a garden full of yellow roses. You and many others. But a single yellow rose at a time.

29
God Loves Pets Too

*N*owhere is God's love closer to us than in the company of our pets.

That is a bold statement. Since there is no record on file anywhere with such a quote from God, a lot of people have the mistaken idea that only they have the honor and privilege of being Souls. But pet lovers know better.

It is an ECK principle that Soul comes to earth in many different states of consciousness—and even in many different body forms. And God loves us all.

Soul exists because God loves It.

While no one can offer indisputable evidence of that love by pulling a quote from some holy text, the proof is in the pudding. God's love is all-encompassing. There is plenty to go around to all creatures.

The stories that follow only include cats, dogs, and turtles to demonstrate that divine love. But don't fret. God's love also includes birds, fish, reptiles, wild animals, and even insects and smaller creatures still.

Lost Collies Come in a Dream
One night a sales representative named Niki had a dream. It was about two collies. Her recollec-

Soul comes to earth in many different states of consciousness—and even in many different body forms. And God loves us all.

165

tion of the dream was a bit garbled the next morning, but she dutifully wrote down as much of it as she could remember. Then she went about her life as usual.

At the dinner table the next day, Niki was surprised when two collies came to the kitchen door. She recognized them immediately.

They were the collies in her dream.

Except for that dream, she might have sent them on their way, thinking they were simply exploring the neighborhood and looking for a handout.

Niki opened the door. Both dogs greeted her like an old friend, and they seemed to be talking to her—trying to tell her something. They nudged her and made moaning sounds. But each refused all treats, food, and water. She got a phone number off one collie's dog tag and left a message for the owner to call her.

In the meantime, Niki grabbed a coat and boots and went outside to be with the collies. They jumped and danced around her, showing complete love and trust.

So she took them for a walk.

Walking up and down the street, she hoped to run into the owner, who might be looking for the lost pets. She tried some commands on them. "Heel!" They obediently fell into step with her. "Stay!" They stayed. "Come!" Of course, they came running up.

Well-trained dogs, she thought.

Finally, the owner got her message and called back to arrange to pick up his dogs. They were delighted at the news. The larger of the two was so happy he began talking like, "Woo Woo Woo!" When the owner arrived, he explained that home was three or four miles away. He was confounded when

Niki was surprised when two collies came to the kitchen door. She recognized them immediately. They were the collies in her dream.

she told him how they had obeyed her commands. They'd never had training, he said.

The lost collies came to Niki's door because they remembered her love from the dream world, where they had already met.

God's love is sufficient for all.

Can Animals Love?

Only a robot or a person new to reincarnation on earth would say no if asked, Can animals love? Highly evolved people accept it as a fact. They know it because of their better understanding of how God's love actually works—due to their longer enrollment here in the University of Hard Knocks.

Yes, animals can love. There are too many such examples of animal behavior to doubt it. Love goes beyond instinct.

Love goes beyond instinct.

Although they are capable of showing love, animals—like many humans—can also show a strong dislike. That can change, however.

A mother took her two daughters, ages eight and ten, to a pet store and returned home with a grey tabby kitten, Socks. All went well for several weeks. Then her son, who had moved to a new apartment where pets were not allowed, brought over his cat, Spook.

Spook took an instant dislike to the kitten. At every opportunity, Spook hissed and swatted at Socks, which soon produced a bloody nose. But it got worse. One day the family had to nurse the kitten back to health because Spook's claw had injured Socks's eye, causing an infection.

In time, though, the two cats became inseparable friends. They did everything together.

Then Spook had a litter of kittens. Socks became a second mother to them: licking them, keeping vigil with Spook over them, even babysitting when Spook left for a drink, food, or just time off. Day after day, Socks stood in during Spook's break times.

The family later came across an article in the newspaper about whether animals can love. With such a pure example of it in their own home, this family has its own answer. Could there be any doubt?

Where Have All the Turtles Gone?

Valerie left cold Illinois one November to visit a retired friend in Florida. A small pond graces his backyard.

He complained to her that his pond, once home to thirty-five turtles, now had no turtles at all. "Where have all the turtles gone?" he asked on several occasions.

At her initial touch, the turtle had panicked. But she softly sang HU, the ancient love song to God, which soothed its fearful struggling.

A couple of weeks into the visit, he suggested a bike ride along the harbor and the lake, where they had ridden the previous year. This bike path ends near a busy road. There, she suddenly felt a presence. Only fifteen feet from the road sat a very large turtle, which let her approach without any sign of fear.

Then a picture from the past flashed through her mind.

She knew this turtle. They'd met the previous year, after a car had run over it, cracking its shell and leaving it on the road with serious injuries. Valerie had gently moved it out of harm's way, setting it in some grass. At her initial touch, the turtle had panicked. But she softly sang HU, the ancient love song to God, which soothed its fearful struggling.

So the turtle now recognized her. It was a meeting between two old friends.

But the road was still a dangerous place for a turtle. Valerie picked up her fifty-pound friend, bicycled with this enormous load under her arm through a park amid unbelieving stares, and took it to her friend's place. The next day, Valerie also found its mate and reunited them. Both soon had a new home in the backyard pond. A much safer place for breeding turtles.

Twice now, God's love showed itself to her turtle friend through her acts of kindness.

Zeke Finds Freedom

Bob had a very old dog, Zeke, who was his special friend. The veterinarian had bad news, though. The fourteen-and-a-half-year-old dog had cancer in his abdomen. No pain. He'd probably just peacefully slip away.

However, if Zeke developed a breathing problem, the vet said it would be time to let him go.

That sad day soon came. Bob and his wife took him to the vet and had Zeke put to sleep. Zeke was in Bob's arms when he went, literally leaping from that tired old body like a prisoner set free from his cell.

On the drive home, Bob's Spiritual Eye opened. He saw Prajapati, the ECK Master who cares for the animals, standing on a hill near a tree. Behind him came a stream of bright golden sunlight from the sky. But there was also a ball of light, and Bob knew instinctively that it was his departed friend, Zeke, in the Soul body. Zeke's joy was unbounded.

By telepathic voice, Zeke said to Bob, "Daddy, I'm free! Thank you for all the love."

By telepathic voice, Zeke said to Bob, "Daddy, I'm free! Thank you for all the love."

*   *   *

Is God's love even sufficient for animals? Yes, it very clearly is—at least it is to those who have the eyes to see and the spiritual awareness to recognize this eternal truth.

30
Grow or Go

We face choices. Like a train, we move forward, stand still, or move backward. Healers know two parts of this as fight or flight. In a vocation, perhaps, it's grow or go. But all three parts of the spiritual life read: unfold, hold, or fold.

Best here, in short, is grow or go.

That's a dilemma every member of Eckankar faces at some time. The bright vision of spiritual freedom, love, and truth fades—and darkness falls. The dark night of Soul.

Then what?

The Spiritual Exercises of ECK done with special diligence will bring one to a new level of God's Light and Sound.

We face choices. Like a train, we move forward, stand still, or move backward.

Ideals

Albert Einstein, the physicist, said, "The ideals which have always shone before me and filled me with the joy of living are goodness, beauty, and truth. To make a goal of comfort or happiness has never appealed to me; a system of ethics built on this basis would be sufficient only for a herd of cattle."

Now consider the ancient truth: When the student is ready the Master appears.

A true follower of ECK is ready to discover the ideals of goodness, beauty, and truth. His Spiritual Eye opens. The Master appears to him in the outer and inner worlds, although unseen by others.

At the 1999 ECK Worldwide Seminar in Minneapolis, two people were overheard in conversation after the Master's Saturday night talk.

The woman said, "Oh, talking about budgies. Really not very spiritual!"

Agitated, and left with little defense, the man replied, "Well, I told you not to expect a fire-and-brimstone sermon."

She: "Yes, but budgies?"

With more agitation, he: "Well, the man speaks in parables, just like Jesus did." And they drifted out of range, her reply lost to hearing.

His noble effort to defend the Master met with a stone wall of self-importance. Someday, she too will be ready for the treasures of living: goodness, beauty, and truth. They spring from love. And then the Master will appear to her, without apology. His love abides, even now. Grow or go.

A true follower of ECK is ready to discover the ideals of goodness, beauty, and truth. His Spiritual Eye opens.

Aim, or Perseverance

An Italian proverb reads, "It is not enough to aim. You must hit."

A Higher Initiate was leaving an office building, as two men stepped out of a sales office behind her. They were in midconversation. One said to the other, "I'm discouraged and encouraged. Discouraged that there's a problem with sales. But encouraged that it's intermittent. And if it's an intermittent problem with sales, I'm going to sell those things!"

Do more than aim at your ideals. Rebazar Tarzs once described it as a drowning man's desire for air.

Those with a true desire for Sugmad, the God of all, will find It. The rest stumble in the night looking for the Mahanta's Light. Always it is so and will be as long as time endures. All must grow or go. Spiritual unfoldment brings change, or growth. All others go on, treading on the endless Wheel of Life until the day the Master appears.

Those with a true desire for Sugmad, the God of all, will find It.

Causes and Effects

Herman Melville, author of *Moby Dick*, knew the reality of karma.

"We cannot live only for ourselves," he said. "A thousand fibers connect us with our fellow men, and among those fibers, as sympathetic threads, our actions run as causes, and they come back to us as effects."

A dear Soul, a Higher Initiate, suffered for years from migraine headaches. They sometimes caused her to be curt with people. Others had no idea of the presence or severity of her headaches, as she generally tried not to mention them.

In contemplation she finally learned the cause of her migraines. She was a direct person. In past lives she dealt with opponents in the most direct way possible by going for their heads with the sword. That aggressive behavior was the reason for her migraines.

Her family finally moved. The barometric pressure in their new location saw fewer drastic swings—much more comfortable for her condition.

In addition, she determined to quit using the medicines for her headaches.

She was nearly out of her mind from the pain

for three months. Shorter bouts of pain recurred. But finally, after a year, the headaches stopped. The family's move to a new geographical location helped; she's finally free of the migraines. She'd dealt with the cause.

The effects, however, linger.

At an ECK seminar she saw the perfect workings of the ECK, Divine Spirit. Some old friends ignored her. Apparently, there were two reasons for it: one, they'd had a run-in with her sword in a past life; and two, she'd been blunt with them in this lifetime as she grappled with the migraines. The ECK let their reactions be a mirror of her own behavior. Though in great pain, she'd sometimes ignored them.

Payback time.

The spiritual exercises and the Mahanta's love showed her an escape from the physical pain. However, old misunderstandings and slights will take longer to disappear from the screen of consciousness. But they will. Only phantoms of the past, they will fade soon enough.

Grow or go.

The spiritual exercises and the Mahanta's love showed her an escape from the physical pain.

Kindness

Loving God means serving others.

Clergyman John Hall said, "Kind looks, kind words, kind acts and warm handshakes—these are secondary means of grace when men are in trouble and are fighting their unseen battles."

Two ECKists joined in the laughter and good-natured kidding of two airline pilots seated near them in a restaurant. A mechanical failure on their passenger jet had nearly caused a tragedy on landing. Only the captain's expert handling of the aircraft brought them in safely with no injury or loss of life.

The pilots had been laughing and joking to release the tension of the past few hours.

One ECKist got a prompting from the Mahanta. "Share the HU with them, Bob." So Bob and his companion rustled up two of the small HU cards. Bob told the pilots about HU, the love song to God, and how singing HU can bring help and comfort in trouble. Both took a card. Each was ready for it.

The ECKists, in love and kindness, showed these two men how to deal with future hazards of their profession. Souls who love God give to others.

Grow or go.

The Spiritual Exercises of ECK, like the HU song, are a mainstay for those who love Sugmad. Divine love, then, brings the fruits of a spiritual life: goodness, beauty, and truth.

And at the root of all is Soul's desire for freedom.

Souls who love God give to others.

31
Sharing What You Love

*H*igher Initiates in California were getting ready to do a workshop. But they wanted a fresh way to think of "serving others." The Mahanta guided their thoughts to serving in terms of sharing their love and enthusiasm with others. So they put the idea of sharing their love into the workshop's title.

Nothing had changed outwardly; they were still giving service to Sugmad (God) and others, but now they had a new focus of where they were coming from.

Now they could speak about the ECK teachings with a new enthusiasm. It made all the difference to their presentations.

You may wish to try this technique in your own ECK Vahana endeavors.

"Susan" was an ECKist who'd just returned from a major ECK seminar. She abounded with love. There simply was no way to hide it. A few days after the seminar, she kept an appointment at her chiropractor's for a back injury she'd suffered before the seminar.

He easily read her high spirits. When he asked how she was, she replied, "Great! I just got back

Now they could speak about the ECK teachings with a new enthusiasm.

177

from the Eckankar Worldwide Seminar, where I got my batteries recharged."

The Mahanta had already prepared the way.

Her doctor said he'd heard about Eckankar before, and they joked about the challenges of living one's beliefs. And that was that.

Two and a half weeks later, the doctor and his wife turned up at the monthly ECK Worship Service. They'd heard about Eckankar years ago but were hesitant due to a bad experience with another spiritual group they'd once been involved in.

He had told his wife about Susan. "She's an ECKist," he said. "She's no flake." So they decided to come to the worship service.

A week later, the couple became ECKists.

Bill is a second example of one who tells others about the ECK teachings by sharing his love. He's employed in a bustling office that leaves little opportunity to tell others about ECK while carrying out his duties.

So how does he manage to share his love for ECK with businesspeople he meets during the course of his day without being pushy about it?

So how does he manage to share his love for ECK with businesspeople he meets during the course of his day without being pushy about it?

He sends them a copy of my book *The Language of Soul.*

The observations of those he's heard back from are most favorable. An accountant at a national certified-public-accountants firm faxed him this message:

"I received your gift in the mail today after we spoke. Thank you—it is exactly what I needed! I was thinking about getting a book that would help me center on a daily basis and am anxious to begin using it."

The Mahanta is also preparing her way.

Bill sent *The Language of Soul* to a dozen friends and relatives too. They've likewise responded with some wonderful feedback.

So that's how Bill shares his love with others.

You likely share your love and enthusiasm for the ECK teachings in your own special way. Sometimes, a shift in focus inside you—like from *service* to *sharing your love*—may mean all the difference to you and others.

So share your love, and see it return to you in many small and unsung ways. In doing so, you become a more finely tuned instrument for the Mahanta.

And for the Sugmad too.

A shift in focus inside you—like from service *to sharing your love—may mean all the difference to you and others.*

32

Who You Are
Speaks Loudly

*I*f you don't know where you are going, you might end up someplace else," said Yogi Berra, the New York Yankees baseball player. His logic has confounded better minds than yours or mine.

So you need a goal in your spiritual life too. Yes, the big one is God-Realization—but how does one get there from here?

By setting little in-between goals.

A God-Realized individual is simply a Co-worker with God. A Co-worker. Yet co-working means to do numerous tasks for the good of all life—one here, one there, a few at a time. The experience gained along the way gives us a lot of rich spiritual insight and understanding.

Oprah Winfrey, the TV star, says, "Doing the best at this moment puts you in the best place for the next moment." That's a very spiritual goal.

A Co-worker with God does that.

William J. H. Boetcker, a Pennsylvania preacher, said in a 1916 pamphlet: "You cannot help men

Co-working means to do numerous tasks for the good of all life—one here, one there, a few at a time.

181

permanently by doing for them what they could and should do for themselves."

That's also a goal in the right direction.

An ECK initiate had a dream early in the year about a coming opportunity to serve as a Co-worker with the Mahanta. In the dream she received a letter. As she opened the white envelope, a living, pulsing six-pointed star emerged from the inside, glowing white and gold. Its brilliance nearly blinded her.

She knew it was an invitation to serve as a RESA, a Regional ECK Spiritual Aide, for the Mahanta, the Living ECK Master. However, since it was still only the dream invitation, she awaited an outer confirmation.

More than half a year later she received it: a letter from RESA Services. It said that a longtime RESA was stepping down. Would she be the new regional leader? Though the dream had foretold this offer, she felt very unsure of her abilities. So she asked the Mahanta for a sign.

That afternoon this prospective RESA was to pick up special dog food from a distributor an hour away.

Ahead on the freeway a large truck was pulling up a hill. Big letters on its side read, "Operation Blessing." She also caught a glimpse, in passing, of the faces of children and adults. Other words spoke of feeding the starving people of the world.

She recognized this waking dream as a sign from the Mahanta, the Living ECK Master: Operation Blessing.

The RESA position would allow her to help even more in giving spiritual food to Souls in this world. To help them help themselves. His mission and hers were to show Souls the way home to God. With this

The RESA position would allow her to help even more in giving spiritual food to Souls in this world. To help them help themselves.

sign on the truck, she knew it was a goal she could pursue with all her heart.

"If you don't know where you're going . . ."

If allowed, the Master will show you the next step, the next, and all the rest.

The Art of Spiritual Dreaming, by myself, is a book full of spiritual food. Because it can show seekers a more direct way home to God, another ECK initiate, Carol, determined to do all in her power to tell people about it. The book is a means whereby people can help themselves find their own way to the blessings of life.

Carol and Doug were to give a public workshop on this dream book in a Borders bookstore in the Minneapolis area. So Carol wondered how best to tell people about the workshop.

She decided to put posters in other stores in the mall. Frankly, when she saw the huge size of those stores, her courage failed. There were no posters in any of the windows. They'd never allow an ECK poster.

Then a thought came to mind of something she'd learned years ago: ask permission to post it in the staff lounge. This approach met with much success.

At the first store, she said, "I'm doing a workshop at Borders on Thursday. Do you have a place I can post this, like a staff lounge?"

The man looked at the poster and said, "Sure, we'll put it in our lounge. What's spiritual dreaming?"

"It's a dream that helps you in some way."

"And helps you help others?" he added.

She said yes, and he strode off to post the poster.

Carol reports the same success in twelve other stores, including a liquor store. She remembered the words of the Master in a talk once, "You are a

She knew it was a goal she could pursue with all her heart.

spiritual being." All the shop owners and managers were too. That was lesson one.

Lesson two came from a workshop presentation by a well-traveled speaker some days before the ECK dream book workshop. Carol noted he was very slick. He'd given the same talk so often that the small audience was putty in his hands. But his talk lacked life for that very reason.

Who we are, our beingness, speaks as loudly as what we say (or louder).

Lesson two: who we are, our beingness, speaks as loudly as what we say (or louder).

Lesson three came after observing Allen and Linda Anderson's presentation at the Mall of America in Minneapolis. They are the coeditors of *Angel Animals: Exploring Our Spiritual Connection with Animals*. Carol noted a great feeling of warmth and community at their book presentation.

Allen and Linda let people in the audience tell stories as the main part of the presentation. Friends greeted attendees, filmed the event, made the food, and brought flowers, says Carol.

Lesson three? Let them serve, as the Master wrote in a recent issue of the *RESA Star*, a publication for RESAs.

So Carol and Doug also let others help with the same tasks at their workshop on *The Art of Spiritual Dreaming*. Many came, many learned.

Carol's observations about the book are that it is giving a special secret out to the world—the Dream Master and the ECK teachings. She is grateful for the chance to be a part of it.

And don't worry, Yogi: Carol, Doug, and many other ECKists know where they're going. And Oprah, they're doing their very best at this moment and will be in the best place for the next.

Who they are speaks louder than words.

Spiritual Exercise: The Open Heart

In this spiritual exercise, you practice keeping an open heart throughout everyday life. It's very tough; I have to work at it all the time too.

No one technique will work for everyone, but there are ways to keep your attention on having an open heart. Start with something you can love, even a pet or a plant, and just love it a lot. As the love comes, let it pour through you.

The habit of love is catching; it builds, gains momentum, and becomes easier. But like a plant that needs watering and loving care every day, the habit of love takes constant attention.

Love won't come through unless the heart is open. To work with an open heart is to love or care for something or someone more than you do for yourself. This is the first step to the divine love that we are looking for.

Start with something you can love, even a pet or a plant, and just love it a lot. As the love comes, let it pour through you.

Ask yourself, "What little step can I take today that will give me a trifle more freedom when I awaken tomorrow?"

CHAPTER SEVEN

Success in ECK

33
From the Master's Chair

$\mathcal{S}$ome little kid may tilt his head far back to take in the whole of an adult towering high over him and think, *What's the weather like up there?*

A new—and not even so new—chela (spiritual student) in ECK may entertain a similar question about the Mahanta, the Living ECK Master. What *is* the weather like up there? A full answer would be impossible to convey, of course, because it's impossible to pass to someone else all the fine points of one's own hopes, fears, pains, joys, and the like. One can only pass along an approximation of what the weather is like where we stand.

So in that light, I'll try to share a few musings about the many chelas in ECK, including you, and what it takes to reach the heart of God.

Let's start with the training of a chela so he may someday enter the inner circle. I'm here talking about those initiates whose spiritual training for the ECK Mastership goes into high gear, the inner circle.

What is among the first lessons a candidate must master?

In a word, PATIENCE.

What is among the first lessons a candidate must master? In a word, PATIENCE.

The word jumps right out at you, doesn't it? Patience. It's a hard one to learn. The dictionary says that one who is patient bears pains or trials calmly or without complaint. See? The bar is set high. But don't worry; the Mahanta, the Living ECK Master knows you can't learn patience all at once, and he doesn't expect it all at once. After all, he once tackled that bear too. It can be a long, hard fight.

So like a gourmet chef, he adds the lessons you need in patience just a few at a time—like the chef adding basil to the soup in a carefully measured amount.

Your sorrows are my sorrows. No, I don't usually take them on, because that'd be to accept your karma. It may be that you need the karma responsible for your sorrow, to become more pure and spiritual at heart. For me to take on karma you need yourself would be to rob you of exactly that bunch of experience needed to let you become more godlike. Your goal is to enter into the heart of God.

Rest assured, however, the Mahanta, the Living ECK Master will lift all unnecessary burdens from you when they're no longer needed.

Let's look at another quality you need to develop on the way to ECK Mastership: HUMILITY.

Perhaps humility should be set in very small type to acknowledge what it's all about. What does the dictionary say? One who seeks humility must "destroy the power, independence, or prestige of___." It leaves us to fill in the blank ourselves. All right, then, let's do it.

To "destroy the power, independence, or prestige of" the ego. Yes, that old, troublesome companion on life's highways and byways. It's the fellow who lands us in so many dark alleys.

Another quality you need to develop on the way to ECK Mastership: HUMILITY.

So out with him!

Unfortunately, that's easier said than done. Ego is like an unwelcome houseguest. He doesn't take hints. And he messes up the place.

So what's the plan? How do we go about kicking out this nuisance?

Here's a strategy that gets some results, but it also attracts clutter—other problems like anger, frustration, a desire for revenge, you name it. First, let your financial reserves fall until there's no other recourse than to accept a job. Any job. Chances are that your supervisor will know all there is to know about the job and you know nothing.

What's more, it's soon apparent it would take a couple of years to gain his level of proficiency. So you're stuck: you're hungry; you must eat.

You could have shuffled off to the welfare line, but you chose to do the responsible thing, to earn your own way because you're able. (Save welfare for a real emergency. It's your ace in the hole in really bad times.) You choose to work because you know the power is in you to find your own way, with a little help here and there from the Master, of course.

To be in such a workplace assures you of getting a good share of humble pie.

But that's a clumsy way to acquire humility. It'll beat you down, chew you up, and spit you out.

There's a better way to go about it—yes, the Spiritual Exercises of ECK. They will open you to the all-inclusive love, wisdom, and power of the ECK to guide you into conditions best suited for your spiritual good.

That's how the ECK Masters learned to subdue the ego during their years of preparation for ECK Mastership.

The Spiritual Exercises of ECK will open you to the all-inclusive love, wisdom, and power of the ECK to guide you into conditions best suited for your spiritual good.

The big question of an outsider would be: Why did they even bother to tackle patience and humility, among a host of other, like qualities? What was in it for them?

Again, it was to earn the right to enter into the very heart of Sugmad (God) Itself, the Ocean of Love and Mercy.

The third divine quality is LOVE. Life provides us with lots of opportunities to become love itself, pure love beyond all telling.

So the third divine quality we'll speak of here is LOVE: divine love, a love excelling. Life provides us with lots of opportunities to become love itself, pure love beyond all telling. It's by way of human love. It smooths out all the wrinkles in our spiritual complexion. Moreover, this love reaches out to the animal world. We learn to see the Light and Sound of God manifesting in the animal world as surely as it shows up in the world of people.

When we're ready to take on spiritual love in addition to human love, the Mahanta, the Living ECK Master sees it and knows it. He opens the floodgates a bit more.

Soon you're in the middle of a whole new area of enrichment. You, too, begin to see and know more about the mysterious ways of God's love working out in the manifestations of all creation.

*   *   *

So that's a bit of what it looks like from the Master's chair.

Admittedly, there are universes upon universes of things to see and know beyond this glimpse here, but patience, humility, and love are certainly cornerstones of the spiritual life of an ECK Master.

That's all for now from the Master's chair.

34

In God's Time
and in God's Way

An ECKist we'll call Al was working one day when a long sliver drove under his fingernail. The only tweezers at home was one with a blunt end, but it wouldn't grip the sliver.

He lived in a small town that had no doctor. Al wished to avoid the time and expense of going to one in a distant town. So what could he do?

Then a simple picture came into his mind that said, "Vet." Of course. He'd go to the town veterinarian to see whether he had a sharp-nosed tweezer. In fact, the vet had one to sell. With it, Al was able to extract the long sliver with the least expense and loss of time.

Had a spiritual force come into play, a beneficial force that let him see the picture of "vet"?

What *had* happened? Was this a so-called miracle?

Al knew. "Just one of the countless 'miracles' that are orchestrated by the Mahanta every day. They come as nudges, images, warm feelings, thoughts, quiet voices. They are the presence of the Mahanta. The Light and Sound acting in my life."

Was this one of the countless 'miracles' that come as nudges, images, warm feelings, thoughts, quiet voices?

193

But there's more.

"From another angle," he wrote, "the experience said when things are painful and unmanageable— be still, be watchful, and get the better tool."

What sage advice. At heart, it tells how to be in agreement with the divine force.

> All is in God's time and
> in God's way,
> no matter what we think or say.

ECKists do know, of course, that Sugmad, the Supreme Being, never intervenes in the minute workings of creation. Instead, it is the Holy Spirit (the Voice of God, the ECK) which is responsible for all miracles that occur. It is a spiritual, creative force.

The Holy Spirit (the Voice of God, the ECK) is responsible for all miracles.

Very often It manifests through the Godman, the Mahanta. He is the embodiment of the ECK.

A chela (spiritual student) once complained she was having no experiences like Soul Travel, dreams, or any sign of spiritual improvement in her life. She concluded that the ECK teachings weren't for her.

It turned out that she wasn't doing the Spiritual Exercises of ECK at all. So she was getting back only what she was willing to put into the ECK teachings: nothing.

Remember that wishing doesn't make it so.

There is an interplay between divine will and human will. Human destiny is written on soft sandstone. In many cases human, or free, will can alter one's individual destiny. The best way, though by no means the only way, is the ECK way.

Success in lifting oneself out of longstanding and hopeless circumstances begins with the Spiritual Exercises of ECK. So honor them, do them.

A new way of life awaits you, but you must take

a firm hand in achieving it.

Then the title "In God's Time and in God's Way" will have meaning for you. Miracles are an expression of that.

Joe, we'll call him, is a black employee on the East Coast of the U.S. He is highly skilled in putting together fast Internet server components, which was his job at the time. He was to travel to Nigeria on business with Paul, a company vice president, on a certain date.

But a change in the schedule caused a serious conflict. Joe had made a commitment to serve at an ECK retreat that same weekend.

Joe was torn. How could he break a spiritual commitment to ECK? Yet his company needed him. What should he do? After much inner struggle, Joe decided to go to Nigeria with Paul.

"It's all service for the Sugmad," he said. "Spiritual or business, it all depends on your attitude."

In his bedroom at home, on the night of departure, Joe felt a prompting to take along the ECK book *The Slow Burning Love of God*. On the London-to-Nigeria leg of the flight, Joe learned the reason. A fellow passenger across the aisle was absorbed in *The Slow Burning Love of God* too.

Joe whispered to him and waved his own book. Soon they were in adjacent seats, engaged in a spiritual conversation.

It'd been time for the stranger to learn about ECK. Joe, an open channel, was a natural instrument for the seeker's golden opportunity. It was one of those "miracles."

That was the trip's first miracle.

The second one took place at their destination in Lagos, Nigeria. Joe and Paul had put in a long

A new way of life awaits you, but you must take a firm hand in achieving it.

day at the company's Lagos office, so they decided to head for the beach. After a while, Paul suggested they leave; it was getting dark. In that part of the world there were perhaps ten thousand black skins for every white one. Paul is white.

Their taxi became snarled in downtown traffic. Even blacks are afraid to go downtown at night because of the many gangs there who rob people.

Suddenly, a gang of eight young men accosted them. They looked hard at Paul. They sounded so polite that Joe failed to take them seriously for a moment. Then he saw they meant business. His money flew out of his pockets and into their hands.

But the gang wanted more money than he and Paul had given them. They threatened to break into the car and beat them.

Joe shut his eyes and began to sing HU, an age-old prayer to God. In seconds, the gang had disappeared.

Joe shut his eyes and began to sing HU, an age-old prayer to God. In seconds, the gang had disappeared. Joe and Paul sat spellbound. Traffic opened, and they were on their way. That was Paul's introduction to the teachings of ECK.

It was the trip's second miracle.

To experience "In God's time and in God's way," do everything in your power to help yourself. Then let the Mahanta do the rest.

35
The Lion and the Ass

*O*ften in the past I've recounted for you one of Aesop's fables. It's time for another.

One day a lion was walking in the forest. All the animals cleared a path and bowed to him in reverence. All but one, that is. An ass brayed a note of derision.

A sudden anger nettled the king of beasts, and he quickly looked around for the source of derision. When he saw it was only the ass, the lion ignored him. Instead, he continued on his way. He didn't even bother to claw the ass for his disrespect and ignorance. For an ass?

Aesop's moral: do not resent the remarks of a fool; ignore them.

* * *

So what brought up the telling of this fable?

ECK chelas have reported the case of a well-respected higher initiate who tells them to take a break from the Spiritual Exercises of ECK. This advice caused them confusion.

This higher initiate has tried taking on the spiritual responsibility of the Mahanta, the Living ECK Master.

Do not resent the remarks of a fool; ignore them.

197

Chelas were advised to do the Spiritual Exercises less often. They were not necessary as a daily routine. In fact, harm could thus be done, was the received perception of the chelas.

Now I wonder how the higher initiate found that out? By reading in *The Shariyat-Ki-Sugmad*? Surely not.

The Shariyat, Book Two, is very clear about both the reason for the Spiritual Exercises of ECK as well as the frequency of practice. It reads:

> The ideal is not to discover the original self, but to allow Soul Its own recognition. . . .

> This recognition comes through the *daily routine* [italics added] of the ECK spiritual exercises.

Could it be any clearer?

Like a high-school sophomore giving the "inside scoop" to a freshman on opening day, some ECK initiates have dispensed other such half-baked ideas as cutting back on the spiritual exercises to reduce the Sound Current of God.

Can you imagine such a thing?

Souls spend lifetimes in search of God's Light and Sound. So when they finally are ready for them, a sophomore (the literal meaning of it is "wise fool") comes along and tells them how to disconnect from the Word of God. What's wrong with this picture?

It's this: Why not let the Mahanta, the Living ECK Master handle the amount of Sound Current that enters into a chela's (spiritual student's) being?

Yes, some ECKists overdo contemplation. They, in unbridled enthusiasm, wish to spend hours at it—in the meantime at the neglect of duty to family and others. Rather, let a chela seek out an ECK

The Shariyat is clear about the reason for the Spiritual Exercises of ECK as well as the frequency of practice.

Spiritual Aide and speak of his spiritual difficulties there. While the ESA may not give a direct answer or suggest a change in doing the spiritual exercises, the Master surely will.

But the higher initiate spoken of above did not wait for others to come, but made it a mission to go forth to bray his ignorance about the spiritual exercises to all within earshot.

Be more the noble lion, less the foolish ass.

The Shariyat, Book Two, does acknowledge that "prolonged contemplation may cause tiredness of body and mind, leading to drowsiness and sluggishness." But its advice is quite the opposite of doing them less. Instead, the recommendation is for the ECK initiate to seek out a quiet place like an isolated room, an orchard, hilltop, or garden.

Be more the noble lion, less the foolish ass.

There one may more easily attune the body with the mind and become rhythmic with Soul.

A side point of deep interest, it says, is to remember that the life-giving part of the air inhaled is not chiefly the oxygen, but the ECK. (This is a seed for contemplation, is it not?)

I must further add one last caution from *The Shariyat*, Book One, about listening to bad advice in regard to the spiritual exercises. Here's the whole quote:

> The Kal Niranjan keeps men blinded to their own higher interests through the five passions. This particular passion, moha, or attachment, is the king of procrastination. It keeps the chela from attending to his spiritual interests, the Spiritual Exercises of ECK.

It bears mention that not everyone who heard the advice to practice the spiritual exercises less often took it. Some, students of *The Shariyat*, knew better. Others, however, took the errant advice gladly. It suited them.

Did moha have anything to do with it?

The ECK Master Rebazar Tarzs says, "The Voice of God is man's divine link with the Almighty Sugmad." Who would even think about cutting off another Soul from Its maker? Only the Kal and his cohorts.

* * *

A former Methodist minister, now retired, is a member of Eckankar. That dear Soul does the spiritual exercises every morning. He sees the Blue Light and sometimes a yellow-white light. That's the Light of God.

The Sound of God comes to him as a ringing. He counts both the Light and Sound with a heart full of joy and gratitude.

* * *

This insight helped her again focus on the real important thing in life— to remember the heart. To bathe in the joy of giving true service to others.

Another ECK chela felt the pressure of stress at home and work. In contemplation, she saw it was a lot of self-imposed stress. Later she discussed this with her husband, also a Higher Initiate.

He helped her see that she loved to help people. Even if only a smile. Somewhere and sometime in the workplace, she'd lost sight of the first love for others. Instead, she'd become task oriented. A project took on more importance than the people doing it. This insight helped her again focus on the real important thing in life—to remember the heart. To bathe in the joy of giving true service to others.

So she's added a new line to her regular declaration of being an open channel for the Holy Spirit:

"Bless this day, and those I serve."

She has recaptured the heart and spirit of the reason for living.

*   *   *

Yes, the Spiritual Exercises of ECK are vital to your unfoldment. So be the lion, not the ass.

36
Oh, You've Come So Far!

*T*he host of a call-in radio program calls himself an expert on dreams. He is a psychia-
trist. Callers' questions about a strange or haunting
dream are grain for his mill.

Most dreams are easy fixes for him. They express some unconscious wish or feeling of the
dreamer. For me, the most interesting part of the
program is the questions. The host's answers often
hit a wall, though, or dribble off into a self-satisfying
string of mumbo jumbo. The show conveniently airs
before bedtime. The few times I braved a segment
of it, it put me in a mood to sleep.

Recently, a caller told of a dream that baffled
this dream expert. The expert, an authority, would
not—could not—admit that it mystified him too,
that it was beyond his area of expertise.

Most of you would have immediately known this
dream for what it was. It was a vivid past-life
experience.

This dream had recurred many times over the
last twenty years and was notable in that it always
replayed battle scenes of the American Civil War of
the 1860s. And the dreamer always floated above
them. He could describe the uniforms, the cannons,

*Most of you
would know
this dream for
what it was—
a vivid past-
life experience.*

the horses and their riders, the weather, the soldiers' guns, the officers' swords, and the like. He saw the wounded and the dead. And he could even smell the smoke of cannon fire.

Evidently, dreams of past lives are not in the expert's repertoire of explanations.

Yet he let on that the matter was very clear to him. By some leap of logic I didn't follow, he tied the dream to the caller's childhood on his grandfather's farm. Forget about the caller's you-are-there descriptions of another time and place. To the expert it was all just a subconscious expression of his feelings.

Other questions were brushed aside with wordy tut-tuts. This exchange must have left the dreamer as puzzled as ever, driving him on to seek more satisfying answers from some other source.

The greatest favor we can do for ourselves is to say we don't know when we don't know.

Vast are the worlds of ECK. The experiences we can have within them are more than there are stars in the heavens. Odds are strong—overwhelming—that you will often run into things you could never have imagined.

This physical life has plenty of surprises too. If your spiritual unfoldment is on track, you will many times find yourself saying about an experience or condition, "I just don't know."

But there are also many things you will know. And it's because the Mahanta will show you.

For example, what do you think the dream authority would have made of this dream reported by someone we will call Belle? In the dream state she was visiting friends, sitting in a large, overstuffed chair. They had a huge pet lizard colored like a Gila

The greatest favor we can do ourselves is say we don't know when we don't. But there are many things you will know because the Mahanta will show you.

monster, a large, poisonous reptile found in Arizona, where she was born and briefly lived later.

However, Belle found this pet lizard loving and sweet. She was not afraid of it. It crawled over her shoulder, down her arm, and into her lap. Then it crept up her front and licked her face.

The alarm clock rang. Since it was an odd dream, she made a note of it in her dream journal.

What do you think the dream expert's analysis would have sounded like?

Well, he never would get a chance to air it, because at breakfast that very morning, the Mahanta, the Inner Master, gave Belle its meaning. And it rang so true.

She was at the table eating breakfast, reading the latest issue of *Arizona Highways*. Her attention was captured by a photo of a Gila monster. Alongside it was an article on how medical scientists had discovered that its saliva contained a substance to help balance insulin levels in type 2 diabetics. There is also a new medication on the market made of a synthesized version of this substance.

This was a health warning from the Master. Belle is not a diabetic, but for a full week, she had been craving sweet things.

The warning said, "You're taking in too much sugar." So she said good-bye to the ice cream and cookies.

Here, then, you've met two very different dreamers, with two very different dream advisers. The Mahanta's advice is worlds beyond that of this other self-described expert. So very, very far beyond his.

Look back sometime and see how far you've come in ECK. And it's all because of your love for the Master.

The Mahanta, the Inner Master, gave Belle its meaning. This was a health warning.

37
Why People Don't Find Spiritual Freedom

A pileated woodpecker has been drumming on a tree, and I broke out our tiny 8×23 binoculars to take a look.

Cloudy skies this morning with new snow lightly sprinkled on the dead leaves below my window, so all the colors are grey. This bird is about the size of a crow. Not your ordinary small woodpecker. A bright red crest graces his head, like the crest on top of a Roman soldier's helmet. Busy, busy—eating breakfast. Yet it has freedom, the ability to come and go as it pleases.

Today, breakfast at Harold and Joan's home. Tomorrow? The world's a big place with many trees in it.

People aren't like this pileated woodpecker. They feel a need to come, go, and do as *others* wish them to do. Go to lunch with so and so. It's been a while. If I don't, he'll feel hurt. Or the need to send a holiday card to someone out of duty, which eats away a few precious minutes that could be better spent on TV, or a book, or merely in a chair with folded hands, dozing.

People aren't like this pileated woodpecker. They feel a need to come, go, and do as others wish them to do.

207

People are slaves to their own fears so much of the time. What will people think? Or say? So they live out desperate lives of unhappiness, pressure, and a sense that life is slipping through their fingers.

But what to do about it?

They eventually find their way to the Mahanta, the Living ECK Master and tell him of their slavery. He says, "Look ahead to tomorrow and forget yesterday. But live today to the fullest measure."

Oh, but how? It's too hard. I can't just reclaim the demands upon my time by others. People will call me selfish.

And so they may, but that's the price. Give up your attachment to others' demands upon your time only after looking at the consequences to you. If an abrupt break in relations is likely to cause you too much unpleasantness or distress, go slowly. Step back a little at a time. Let old wounds heal.

And also ask yourself, "What little step can I take today that will give me a trifle more freedom when I awaken tomorrow?"

The best, least shocking way to gain more freedom is to change something only a little bit today.

The best, least shocking way to gain more freedom is to change something only a little bit today. But it has to be something that you can clearly point to tomorrow. Will the new day let you say of the little change made yesterday, "I feel better now"?

From so many angles, with so many methods via the Spiritual Exercises of ECK have I shown people how to find a greater measure of freedom inside themselves. Yet many remain unhappy.

The truth is that their old habits of yesterday offer them more comfort than they could ever face up to. Basically, a change would mean giving up the feelings of being a victim of others and life. They would have to take responsibility for themselves. Oh, they may try out their wings a bit. However, when their initial attempts at taking responsibility for the new effects set in motion by them go sour, who's there to blame for the failure?

Here habit rushes to the rescue again like cavalry at a crisis in battle. It's easier to blame someone else for a plan gone awry than face it themselves.

Responsibility is a lonely thing. In fact, most people are social creatures who choose to stay in situations that hold them as securely as a prison cell. They don't like their misery, exactly. However, it's easier to deal with than the uncertainty brought about by striking out in a new, uncharted direction.

That's the reason people hate change. It means taking responsibility.

So a spiritual guide needs a mountain of patience, giving the message of spiritual freedom in a hundred different ways: through laughter, stories, talks, new spiritual exercises, again, and again, and again. He's as patient as the day is long.

There's no hurry.

He knows that Soul moves toward spiritual freedom at a pace It feels comfortable with and will reach the heights the ECK Masters have gained through their own rugged paths and disciplines a long time ago. There is no hurry in the worlds of God. All is in its right place, at the appropriate time. So relax and let God's hand touch you.

That's the secret to finding the gold of spiritual freedom.

There is no hurry in the worlds of God. All is in its right place, at the appropriate time. So relax and let God's hand touch you.

38
The Spiritual Years of ECK

October 22 marks the Spiritual New Year of ECK. Taking place in autumn, it signifies the high point or spiritual harvest in the year's cycle. It is a time of rededication.

The ECK Spiritual New Year also celebrates the birth date of Paul Twitchell, the modern-day founder of Eckankar. Of more spiritual import, however, is the fact that it was on this day that he accepted the Rod of ECK Power and became the Mahanta, the Living ECK Master.

He came to help people find their way home to God in the most direct way.

So the ECK Spiritual New Year is the beginning of a new, higher cycle for the coming year. Historically, October 22 is the day that the Living ECK Master of the times receives the Rod of ECK Power and begins his spiritual duties.

Each new spiritual year carries a theme. This theme, or name, gives a focus to the spiritual direction and efforts of ECK initiates for the next twelve months.

The ECK Spiritual New Year is the beginning of a new, higher cycle for the coming year.

The Light and Sound of God are central to the ECK teachings, because they, taken together, are the Voice of God, the Holy Spirit.

The cycle of spiritual years begins with "The Year of Light and Sound." The Light and Sound of God are central to the ECK teachings, because they, taken together, are the Voice of God, the Holy Spirit. They form a cosmic wave that goes out from the heart of Sugmad (God) to the ends of creation. This wave is like a wave that comes ashore from the ocean.

Soul needs to catch the wave that returns home to God. The Mahanta, the Living ECK Master's job is to help the individual learn how to do that.

The second year in this cycle is "A Year of Spiritual Healing." After spending many lifetimes in search of truth, the individual is often a bruised and battered wreck. So even after having bathed for a year in the Light and Sound of God, Soul needs a time to heal.

The Spiritual Years of ECK

But life is ever the teacher. So it is necessary to set aside a time of healing every twelve years for the individual to gather strength for the next leg of the spiritual journey.

Third, "The Year of the Shariyat."

The Shariyat-Ki-Sugmad is the body of spiritual writings that form the ECK holy scriptures. It means "Way of the Eternal." These scriptures are located on both the physical and the invisible planes. They contain the secrets that Soul needs to rise above the human passions that keep It in misery or despair. These scriptures cut through the illusions of temporal power.

So the books of the Shariyat-Ki-Sugmad lead Soul to wisdom, spiritual power, and freedom.

Fourth, "Year of the ECK Missionary."

Each person has a mission in life, a purpose. During this annual cycle, the individual tries to learn, then align, his personal mission with that of God's divine plan for each Soul's return home to the Ocean of Love and Mercy. This ocean is the home, or heart, of God.

One then seeks to be in harmony with the flow of life. In other words, the individual puts his attention upon the goal of becoming a Co-worker with God. We are here to learn divine love. Along the way, we learn that our personal mission also means helping others find their way to it.

Fifth, "A Year of HU."

HU is the most ancient name for God. It has provided love and support to Souls from prehistoric times. Early ECK Masters, like Agnotti, taught early humans this word in the dream state.

It is the sacred name of God, not God Itself. HU, the first impulse from the Ocean of Love and Mercy,

Life is ever the teacher. So it is necessary to set aside a time of healing every twelve years for the individual to gather strength for the next leg of the spiritual journey.

is the origin of all motion, force, light, sound, or vibration. One can sing this word to instantly call for spiritual help. It opens one to help from the Holy Spirit.

Sixth is "The Year of Giving."

The entire reason for Soul's journey is to learn the spiritual need for giving. A life of meaning is a life of giving.

The entire reason for Soul's journey is to learn the spiritual need for giving. A life of meaning is a life of giving. Whether of purse or time, true giving is a recognition of the central tenet of life. Namely, Soul exists because God loves It. God's love freely comes to all of us, so we must learn both to accept that love and then to pass it on to others.

The ECK Master Rebazar Tarzs passed this secret to his disciple Peddar Zaskq. "Therefore, if you desire love," he said, "try to realize that the only way to get love is by giving love."

Seventh, "A Year of Blessing."

It's a time to count your blessings. Each day and breath of life is another opportunity to move forward spiritually by increasing our capacity for God's love. Bless each moment, each thought, each word, and each deed. Let only the pure love of God flow from you and into your own universe.

Eighth is "The Year of Thanksgiving."

This year has much in common with the preceding one. Here, however, we are willing to let our joy of life show in a spirit of celebration. In this regard, the American holiday of Thanksgiving is in the right spirit. Enjoy the company of your loved ones at special celebrations of your own choosing throughout the year. Give thanks for the gift of life.

Ninth, "A Year of Creativity."

God's special gift to the higher forms of spiritual evolution is the gift of creativity. It is a reflection of our highest nature. This creativity will be for constructive ends, of course, and shows the progress of Soul in Its quest to become godlike.

This creative power develops through the Spiritual Exercises of ECK. It can be used in every area of your daily life.

Tenth is "Year of the ECK Teacher."

This cycle is opposite to its counterpart, "Year of the ECK Missionary." First, the missionary finds the Souls that are ready for the return home to God. Later, the Arahata, as an aide to the Mahanta, the Living ECK Master, leads a class of people who desire the knowledge of truth found in the ECK teachings. This is a key year.

Eleventh in this cycle of spiritual years is "The Year of Graceful Living."

As people unfold spiritually, their way of interacting with others becomes more graceful. There is an honest attempt to see the Mahanta in every other Soul, because then a graceful life is found to be the natural life. Grace is a balm that makes things run better.

The final and twelfth year is "A Year of Consecration."

It is a time to dedicate yourself anew to *being* a Co-worker with the Mahanta. That is a necessary part of *becoming* a Co-worker with God. This twelfth year in the cycle of spiritual years is a chance to tie up the loose spiritual ends of the last cycle and prepare for the new one next year.

*   *   *

These years will be synchronized to run in order beginning on October 22, 2001. Until then, to finish out this present cycle, the Spiritual Years of ECK will be the following:

As people unfold spiritually, their way of interacting with others becomes more graceful.

- Oct. 22, 1996–Oct. 21, 1997: "A Year of Consecration"

- Oct. 22, 1997–Oct. 21, 1998: "A Year of Creativity"

- Oct. 22, 1998–Oct. 21, 1999: "The Year of Giving"

- Oct. 22, 1999–Oct. 21, 2000: "A Year of HU"

- Oct. 22, 2000–Oct. 21, 2001: "Year of the ECK Teacher"

- Oct. 22, 2001–Oct. 21, 2002: "The Year of Light and Sound"

- Oct. 22, 2002–Oct. 21, 2003: "A Year of Spiritual Healing"

(and so forth)

*   *   *

The names of the spiritual years may change in time to fit the change in consciousness.

The names of the spiritual years may change in time to fit the change in consciousness.

From 1965 on, the 12-year cycles run like this:

- Oct. 22, 1965–Oct. 21, 1977 (years 1–12)

- Oct. 22, 1977–Oct. 21, 1989 (years 13–24)

- Oct. 22, 1989–Oct. 21, 2001 (years 25–36)

- Oct. 22, 2001–Oct. 21, 2013 (years 37–48)

- Oct. 22, 2013–Oct. 21, 2025 (years 49–60), etc.

39
The Breadth and Depth of the ECK Initiation

Of what use is an ECK initiation?

A fable from Aesop shows the advantages in a striking way.

*   *   *

A peacock once met a crane that happened to land in a barnyard. The peacock spread its rainbow of tail feathers to catch the full glory of the sun.

"Look," said he, "what have you to compare with the beauty of my feathers? Why, yours are like the gray of dust."

The crane said not a word. Instead, it spread its wings and flew up toward the sun. "Follow me if you can," he called from the sky.

But the peacock stood among the barnyard fowl, while the crane soared in freedom into the wild blue.

*   *   *

In a word, the ECK initiation offers freedom. Spiritual freedom.

It gives freedom from the material clutchings that try to grasp the tail feathers of an individual

In a word, the ECK initiation offers freedom. Spiritual freedom.

and keep Soul in an earthbound state.

What is the moral of the peacock-and-the-crane story? The useful is of greater importance and value than is the ornamental. In terms of the ECK initiation, it means that while an ECK initiate may appear to be among the lowliest of people, his element is in the heavens. There he resides in joy and freedom.

The ECKist thus holds the key to spiritual liberty. Of such is the ECK initiation.

An irony of the spiritual journey is that in today's society a member of Eckankar may be regarded as a second-class citizen, though he is able to explore the high worlds via Soul Travel. The irony is thus of one who looks poor while rich in a real possession.

Society may mock Soul Travel. Yet it will endorse world travel as an enriching experience that gives a traveler a wealth of understanding and wisdom about people. Travel does do that. But Soul Travel does that and more.

Dreams and contemplation, besides Soul Travel, are inner experiences that offer other keys to understanding one's unconscious likes and dislikes.

Dreams and contemplation, besides Soul Travel, are inner experiences that offer other keys to understanding one's unconscious likes and dislikes.

A woman in ECK was asked to cook food for a company picnic the next day. In spite of poor health, she did so. She'd worn the wrong shoes for a long session in the company's kitchen, and by day's end her body was run down.

Years ago, she had taken to heart a saying. It'd been a guiding star, but now she'd turned aside from it by agreeing to cook food though it went against her wishes.

"Do not merely what you *can* do," ran the saying, "but what *only you* can do."

Her reluctance, however, was set at a deeper level

of past experience. In contemplation, the Mahanta showed her a lifetime as a black slave around the time of the American Civil War. She lived on a southern plantation. Her vantage point was that of a young child too small to see the tabletops, but with a child's-eye view of well-worn floor planks.

There was a sense that her mother lay dying.

In following glimpses, the Master showed her as an orphan to be trained as a kitchen maid. Earlier contemplations had shown her later as a young woman. She carried food such as sweet-potato pie to soldiers when their regiments passed through the area during the war. After the war, she was among the vast number of freed slaves "with nowhere to go and few skills with which to get there," as she put it.

Slavery had left a sour taste toward authority.

Those past-life years of slaving away in a kitchen to feed large groups of people had set a distaste for any kitchen work that involved groups. Another set of ironies is that in this lifetime her mother was the head cook at a small hotel. Her father owned his own bakery.

That upbringing did instill a love and creativity for the preparation of food. So she enjoys cooking in her own kitchen to spoil friends with feasts. It's a choice drawn of love.

Yet cooking for large groups for duty's sake leaves her feeling cold and empty.

The years have flown since her first ECK initiation. Her life's road, as for many of us, has seen countless dips and rises, curves and straight runs, mud, or firm, smooth pavement. That's the outer side of life. It reflects the calm and turmoil of her inner life, an essential part and balance of her

In contemplation, the Mahanta showed her a lifetime around the time of the American Civil War.

whole being as she made her laborious trek along the path to God.

To be sure, the ECK initiations paved the road for the next day's travel.

The passage of time has since watched this woman enter the higher circles of ECK initiations. Her understanding of the workings of all around in relation to herself has likewise seen unbounded growth. She notes how the ECK (Holy Spirit) has washed away the underpinnings of her reality in waves.

"The more we lose," she observes, "the more we learn we can live without anything and everything except the love of God.

"And since that is one thing that will never be denied us, we ought to be happy. But we are not until we have learned to love God in return. And that is why man searches so hard without finding, because he doesn't understand that the key lies within his own heart."

She expresses well the breadth and depth of rich insight that come of the ECK initiations.

Yet there's more.

"I have found the key," she says, "but it is not what I expected. ECKists know that heaven isn't what Christians expect, but I'm sure (the Spirit of) God isn't what most ECKists expect. It brings a profound joy and brightness to my inner world, as if the doors to the innermost of heavens have been flung open and the angel of love bestows Its blessings upon me.

"But as love softens me, it leaves my heart tender to the struggles of others, and I see in their eyes the untold stories of Soul lost, Soul losing, Soul finding.

> *"The more we lose," she observes, "the more we learn we can live without anything and everything except the love of God."*

"I cry for them, with them, as you, the Mahanta, have done countless times for me since I began my journey."

Of such is her realization of the love of God. But is her battle won, the journey over? No, for the true realization of the glory of living and loving takes one to a still greater recognition of Spirit.

Yes, there is more.

"All I want to do, all I can do anymore," she says, "is love life as God loves me and all Souls. I don't often know how, and I doubt my own worthiness. But I've decided that doesn't matter. I simply must love. If it takes me forever to get it right, so be it, as long as I'm always willing.

"Willing to surrender everything, to listen and see in the name of Sugmad [God], and go wherever the Mahanta wants me."

You're not a peacock, but a lucky crane.

Practice talking inwardly to the Master about anything that is in your heart. One day you may be surprised to hear him answer you, loud and clear.

✴ Spiritual Exercise: The Master's Presence

As you sit in contemplation, ask the Inner Master for more understanding of the words *I am always with you.*

Practice talking inwardly to the Master about anything that is in your heart. Visualize him sitting right next to you and establish a dialogue. One day you may be surprised to hear him answer you, loud and clear.

Practice of the Master's presence is one of the four fundamentals of ECK.

Whoever orders his life around an agreement with the Light and Sound of ECK is assured that every problem has a ready-made solution near at hand.

CHAPTER EIGHT

Living in the World

40
Soul Travel and the Continuity of Life

$\mathcal{C}$hristy is a woman from Nigeria with a wonderful story about Soul Travel. Would you like to hear it? All right, then, make yourself comfortable and let's listen.

Her story is a good example of the continuity of life.

It was a military hospital, and Christy, in for an operation, was taken to her ward. The ward officer asked, "Which of the churches do you belong to?" "I am not a Christian," she said.

"What, then, are you?"

"I am an ECKist."

"What is an ECKist?"

"I am in ECKANKAR."

"My God!" he said aghast. "And your name is Christiana." How could anyone with the name Christiana be anything other than a Christian? Christy did everything in her power to make him understand what ECKANKAR was, but their conversation hit a blank wall.

The operation was early the next morning. She was put on a gurney and rolled to the operating

225

room. As she chanted HU and turned the operation over to the Inner Master, the Light of God began to shine strongly in the room.

Then the operation began.

The next moment, Christy was standing on the inner planes with the ECK Masters Lai Tsi, Rebazar Tarzs, Fubbi Quantz, Gopal Das, and myself, the Mahanta, the Living ECK Master. Lai Tsi was the main surgeon.

Christy, in the meantime, was looking at herself on the operating table.

It took the outer doctor four hours to finish the operation. But the ECK Masters hadn't yet completed the inner one. In the interim, she appeared to be in grave danger, so the doctor put a battery of drugs into her.

For her part, Christy, in the Soul body, smiled at the ECK Masters as they were finishing. As they did, she found herself back in the physical body. Her Soul Travel adventure was over.

Her stay in the hospital lasted only ten days, and when she returned home, she was well healed.

And that is what Christy heard and saw.

*   *   *

Christy's story nicely illustrates the ECK principle of the continuity of life, an understanding of which overcomes the fear of death.

Wisdom lies in recognizing the gift of this life. It's a wonderful opportunity for Soul to thrive and unfold spiritually. People are often afraid to live because they're afraid to die. Why go so fast and lose sight of the Spiritual Exercises of ECK?

Doing the Spiritual Exercises of ECK is important because it clears out the impurities in the

Christy, in the Soul body, smiled at the ECK Masters as they were finishing. As they did, she found herself back in the physical body. Her Soul Travel adventure was over.

human consciousness that block awareness of the other planes.

This gift the ECK Masters bring is to allow people to live more fully in God's love. When God's love comes in, fears go out, including the fear of death. And so do all the other passions of the mind. The Spiritual Exercises of ECK put the mind where it belongs. It's a good servant but a poor master.

When God's love comes in, fears go out, including the fear of death.

The spiritual exercises keep the consciousness clear and the heart open to the ECK.

Take a few moments in contemplation each day with the Mahanta, the ECK, and the SUGMAD to keep in touch with this all-important principle—the continuity of life.

41
The Art of Soul Travel

---

*S*oul Travel is both an art and a science. In its purest form, Soul Travel is simply Soul leaving behind Its awareness of the human consciousness and moving into a higher one closer to God. That's all it is.

Yet Soul Travel is more than a nebulous experience, and it has many levels. Sometimes it's only a subtle shifting of consciousness from everyday problems to a sudden commanding overview of how those same problems fit into the divine plan of Soul's evolution to a higher state of purity. Soul Travel ranges far and wide.

Without a shred of doubt, though, Soul Travel means change.

Change.

Most people claim to like change, but their claims are with some strong limitations. Change is good and desirable if it produces conditions that are more comfortable than the present ones. For example, it is a good thing to win the lottery, but it is certainly not good to go bankrupt. We're careful to qualify the sort of change that's acceptable.

But whether we like it or not, change happens. And it happens whether we know the art of Soul

In its purest form, Soul Travel is simply Soul leaving behind Its awareness of the human consciousness and moving into a higher one closer to God.

Travel or don't. So what's the difference?

Soul Travel makes us aware of God's plans.

Can't holy scriptures do that? They can open us to new areas of spiritual understanding, sure, but there's nothing like experience to bring that understanding home and to make it a part of us. Can you imagine a student who studies a book on dancing but never dances? He or she could pass a written test on all the different kinds of dances in the world, but would that produce a skilled and graceful dancer?

Soul Travel makes us aware of God's plans.

Soul Travel is about Soul's journey home to God.

Some of it is taught in books. That's a necessary step in many cases, because often the spiritual student may not be able to travel the world over to find a Master who can teach him the ancient art and science of Soul Travel in person. But books are just a beginning.

So how is Soul Travel an art and how is it a science? The science part of it has to do with book learning, or head knowledge. This is a way of catching the theory of it. It's like learning all about the many forms of dance in the world from a book. A good overview.

The art of Soul Travel comes in actually doing it. That means sitting down at a quiet time of the day, every day, and doing a Spiritual Exercise of ECK.

A spiritual exercise is a form of prayer. It is nothing more than being still and listening for the Voice of God or watching for the divine Light. Both are real. There is nothing imaginary about the Sound and Light of God, as many can attest who have become successful with the Spiritual Exercises of ECK.

Here's a brief one to get started—or to renew yourself if you're an ECKist who has slipped from your spiritual disciplines and now wonders why your inner experiences have stopped:

Find a comfortable place to sit or lie down for twenty minutes. Pick a time when you won't be disturbed. Shut your eyes. Gently focus your attention on a point between your eyebrows—the Tisra Til, the Spiritual Eye. It's a doorway into the higher worlds. Now softly begin singing a word over and over. The word is HU. It's pronounced just the way it looks: "HU" or "hue." Sing it gently, with love and expectation.

What you're expecting is some manifestation of the Sound or Light of God. Either one will be your first step with conscious Soul Travel. You're expecting to become aware of the presence of God.

What could be simpler?

What could be more in keeping with your spiritual purpose on earth?

Soul Travel will eventually show you the purpose of your life here. Some people begin to catch glimpses of their past lives. It's all a part of learning who and what you are as a child of God, and furthermore, it's the natural way of spiritual unfoldment used by true saints over the centuries.

So why is there such an urgency to learn the art of Soul Travel?

The ECK Masters like Rebazar Tarzs teach that earth is the ash can of the universe. No, it doesn't mean that it's a divine blunder of creation. It just means that earth is nearly too perfect a place to get spiritual purification. All the negativity of daily life will get worse before it gets better.

Wars are not going away.

Sing HU gently, with love and expectation. You're expecting to become aware of the presence of God.

In fact, with the unbridled population explosion in recent decades, more and more inexperienced Souls are coming here. They're like children who don't know right from wrong.

So we're seeing people in powerful governments around the world busily breaking all the divine laws of noninterference. Under one pretext or another, usually to save a certain class of people from themselves, these people in government invade the borders of other countries to set things right. The irony is that their own home fences need mending.

This unbridled interference in the domestic affairs of other nations is responsible for the current rise in international terrorism.

The desire for power and control over others creates a backlash. Instead of producing a world culture of peace and stability, it foments wave after wave of retaliatory violence. Well, folks, that's life on this utopia called earth.

Use the spiritual love and wisdom gained from experience with the Light and Sound of God to make this a better place—in spite of the odds.

Some people, the immature Souls, always need to beat up on each other to learn that pain hurts. People of power and control have little in common with people of love and compassion.

They are worlds apart.

The role of spiritually mature Souls in this world is to lift themselves above the melee with the Spiritual Exercises of ECK and the art of Soul Travel. Then use the spiritual love and wisdom gained from experience with the Light and Sound of God to make this a better place—in spite of the odds.

42
Behind the Scenes with Paul Twitchell

$\mathcal{P}$aul Twitchell showed himself to be the master compiler of the scattered wisdom that he brought together in the path we know as Eckankar.

When the ancient mysteries have gone so far afield that only distorted fragments remain in the public mind, then the Order of Vairagi Adepts sends forth a chosen one from among its band to restore truth, such as it is, in the material domain.

Paul had an uncanny knack for depicting the human condition through the writings left by other authors. But he took their efforts a step further. He recast the seed ideas so they fit into a grander, more compelling spiritual framework. He artfully presented the subject of the power of imagination as Soul's peculiar talent for survival in every universe of creation.

It is a curious thing, though, to hear Paul once speak of the Halls of Los in William Blake's poetry when Blake hardly seems to have used this phrase at all.

Paul Twitchell showed himself to be the master compiler of the scattered wisdom that he brought together in the path we know as Eckankar.

233

Blake had made an attempt to demonstrate the seeing power of Soul along the Time Track, yet it is doubtful that he ever got an image of it as concrete as Paul's of the dead conditions of the past, which only spring to life when the light of Soul shines upon them. The closest mention Blake makes of Halls of Los is "Los's Halls." Yet even in doing so, Blake misses the context that puts animation into past lives spent in an otherwise lifeless, dank corridor of time.

So Paul actually captured the image behind Blake's image and set it down as a concrete reality—an image that he isolated and identified as the heart of Blake's gift to spiritual literature.

Los is an important contribution to the font of spiritual doctrine, for this is the creative imagination. The lord of the time-space universes snared Soul and reduced all of Its perceptive powers down to the sensations of the human body. Man thus lost his original freedom out of fear and obedience to external authority, the crippler of the poetic genius that lives within him. The divine imagination is the only faculty that can make one godlike, for it acts in keeping with the laws of ECK (Holy Spirit). Otherwise, man is doomed to the hell of his own little self.

Paul was a proponent of the Law of Economy one must search out in order to have the gathering of forces that occurs in Self- and God-Realization.

Paul was moreover a proponent of the Law of Economy. While it is true that Alice Bailey and other occult writers have put down their opinions of it, Paul was the one who gave concise and clear reasons why one must search it out in order to have the gathering of forces that occurs in Self- and God-Realization.

This law is the divine tension behind all actions and behavior in nature so that no force is ever lost or misspent.

Initiates of the high circles in ECK unfold only to the degree to which they perceive how the Law of Economy governs the orbits of objects in every macrocosmic or microcosmic creation. This includes the cohesive atoms in the human body. This principle is the modus operandi of the ECK Masters, who pursue their missions with simplicity and grace. They reverberate to the Music of God. It compels their every impulse and deed. The greatest benefit is gotten from every expenditure of thought and energy, and whoever orders his life around an agreement with the Light and Sound of ECK is assured that every problem has a ready-made solution near at hand.

Paul swept into the corners and stirred up thought forms that had lain dormant for ages. The knowledge gleaned from the source manuscripts of the Shariyat-Ki-Sugmad is of paramount value to one who aspires to be a Co-worker with God. Indeed, the fountainhead from which the ECK writings spring is the Ancient Gospel compiled by the Nine Silent Ones, whose main duty it is to gather up and sort out the unchanging laws that enfold every ripple in life.

The library alongside the main Wisdom Temple at Sahasra-dal-Kanwal on the Astral Plane is an enormous place of many roomy departments.

In the archival warehouse rests a manuscript drawn from the main text of the Shariyat, which is closely guarded in the nave of the Temple of Asklepposis. Paul, myself, and certain appointed writers do research from this archival material when they are writing their own books. In fact, Paul's firm hand has dotted the left margin of this source manuscript with voluminous notes.

Whoever orders his life around an agreement with the Light and Sound of ECK is assured that every problem has a ready-made solution near at hand.

Paul once told of how the Unknown Masters arrange for the distribution of knowledge to all levels of understanding among people. Each topic in the Shariyat is addressed point by point—but in up to eight or more different ways—and each separate paragraph restates the gist of the core idea for another area of consciousness. Paul and the writers who get into these archives of the secret teachings select the grade of paragraph that most nearly fits the spiritual maturity of their readers.

Paul and other ECK Masters leave priceless gems of insight that await only our determination to make them living ideals, to smooth out our own dealings in life. He told of ways for the self-protection of the body and why these practical methods work.

Yet some critics may say that too much attention is being paid to Paul and the past. Why hark upon yesterday? The present is now.

True, but Paul offered a front-row seat to witness how the ECK brought him through the psychic and mind areas, which have troubled so many of us. His journey ultimately brought him the pure spiritual realization of the Mahanta, which is the natural longing of every Soul, including you.

The ECK teachings reveal the means for unfoldment into the ECK Mastership.

The ECK teachings—both Paul's writings and my own—reveal the means for unfoldment into the ECK Mastership. They are an inspiration to all who feel the flame of God urging them to tell mankind the cardinal truths of ECK.

A man of God is driven by the Spirit of God, the ECK. It is divinely merciless in how It renders the greater consciousness. And should one ever glimpse the Supreme Being Itself, he can henceforth live only within Its Sound and Light. One compromises this delicate relationship only at the risk of spiritual death.

Paul gathered and compressed old esoteric concepts into a single body of writings for later distribution to devotees of God like you. The ECK teachings are hardly encompassed by any earthly manuscript, however, for truth outshines all human understanding. Our measured experience is the final voucher of truth.

At least once a day, therefore, let the Sound and Light of ECK enliven the lower states of your being with spiritual impulses.

The various levels of the mind can overreact to the rush of everyday living and make us tense and angry. A host of other negative traits try to pull us off the spiritual ladder, leaving us on edge and out of sorts. This brings more complications, and we are frantic to find magic elixirs or the cure-all of the philosopher's stone. In our frenzy, we forget that help is as near as a few moments in contemplation with the Inner Master. Empty all problems from the receptacles of your mind, for this meeting with the Mahanta, the Living ECK Master is a blessed sacrament in the Holy of Holies.

Free your mind of complexity and worry, and the silent wind of God will enter the sacred temple of consciousness in your heart. A few silent moments of attention upon the eyes of the Mahanta will calm the turbulence and give you courage. A short period of contemplation can be done anywhere, even in your car in a parking lot.

Once tensions relax, it is just moments before the healing current of ECK begins to restore you.

Fear, doubt, and uncertainty make life a dubious undertaking. As Soul grows in awareness, you

Free your mind of complexity and worry, and the silent wind of God will enter the sacred temple of consciousness in your heart.

will become more definite in what you want from life. That is fruit from the seed of expanding consciousness. It is the legacy of the ECK to you.

43
A Test in a Dream Doctor's Office

The ECK, Divine Spirit, has a marvelous knack for giving spiritual tests to those on the path of truth. It employs a number of ways to spiritually uplift people. If they will stay on the path.

An example of this testing is an experience from the inner planes. It went like this:

In this inner experience the Mahanta, the Inner Master, had an appointment with a very good doctor. It was the first appointment of the day. The doctor immediately began to run a series of tests, after which he prescribed the remedies. All was going well.

Then the door to his office opened, and a whole crowd of patients began to file in. The room was soon full of people. (All were ECKists.) Some were new patients (First Initiates), but others had been with the doctor for many years (longtime members of Eckankar). The atmosphere in the room was cordial and friendly. People chatted about their (spiritual) ills and all the wonderful cures effected by this doctor with a special healing talent. None of them really noticed the Mahanta.

239

In the meantime, the doctor and the Mahanta kept busy.

The crowd began to grow restless, impatient with the long delay before their own appointments. Then, at about the same moment, it occurred to each patient that the room was full of individual patients. They began to count noses. So if it took the doctor this long to finish the first appointment, how long would it be before their turn?

Now the atmosphere in the doctor's office changed to one of anger. People started to fidget and complain.

Whispers began to float through the room: "Why, he's completely unorganized . . . All these people have an appointment for the same time . . . It'll be *hours* before he sees ME!"

It was not a happy crowd.

Yet as bad as things were, they were about to get worse. The doctor himself began to show signs of distress, but not at the dark mood of his patients, who did not make an effort to be discreet with their criticisms. No. Instead, the doctor was showing signs of illness himself.

Unexpectedly, giving no word of explanation, the doctor left his office and did not immediately return.

He interrupted his work to wipe sweat from his forehead. Then his face turned pale. Next, his patients noted that he was shivering, as though the room's temperature had suddenly dropped below the freezing point. Not a good sign.

Unexpectedly, giving no word of explanation, the doctor left his office and did not immediately return.

That made his patients furious. "I'm not used to being treated like this!" said one elderly woman as she stormed from the room. The voice of another man now rose. "At least he could have the decency—," but his complaint was cut off as he slammed the door on his way out. All the other patients made similar complaints and also left. Soon the room was empty.

The Mahanta alone remained. He went into the next room to see the receptionist. He expressed his concern about the doctor's health and left his phone number. "Call me when the doctor is ready to complete the appointment," he said. She smiled as he left the office.

Shortly after that, the phone rang. It was the receptionist.

"The doctor's ready to continue the appointment now." And so the Mahanta and the doctor were able to finish what they had begun.

* * *

What message is the ECK giving through this inner experience?

The Mahanta, the Living ECK Master is the agent of the Sugmad (God), so the Master will always act in keeping with God's Voice, the ECK (Holy Spirit). The Outer Master is the Living ECK Master (the doctor, in this experience). The Inner Master is the Mahanta. In reality, they are one and the same here.

The message of the ECK?

Divine Spirit may use any variety of circumstances to test the spiritual strength of an initiate. That may include the health of the Master.

In this case, It tested all the people in the room at the same time. (Their appointments were for the same time slot.) Also of note is that not all the ECK initiates in the world were involved in the test: only those in the room. They were the problem people,

Divine Spirit may use any variety of circumstances to test the spiritual strength of an initiate. That may include the health of the Master.

or the "propeeps," as Paul Twitchell once so aptly called them. A small part of the ECK membership.

So, as long as these patients in the experience had both the doctor and the Mahanta in the room, they were fairly calm and sociable. But the first appointment was taking too long. When would it be their turn to be the center of attention?

And then the doctor (the Living ECK Master, making fewer public appearances) leaves the room. There goes their chance for recognition.

Oddly, you'll notice, once the doctor leaves, they all forget about the Mahanta. It's as if he's become invisible to them. In fact, he's still there until after the last one has left the room. Leaving the office in anger means leaving Eckankar. It was a spiritual test from the ECK that all the people who had been in the room failed. Their egos demanded a showy exit.

Once these people with deep spiritual problems were gone, the Mahanta and the doctor continued with their appointment.

*   *   *

On a billboard on the grounds of an elementary school is a message that applies here. It reads:

NEVER
NEVER
NEVER
GIVE UP

Once these people with deep spiritual problems were gone, the Mahanta and the doctor continued with their appointment.

44
The Spiritual
Lie of Socialism

*I*n the United States, the beautiful story of Thanksgiving has evolved from an entirely different reality in history.

The story is about European settlers in North America. For example, when Plymouth Colony was established in the bitter winter of 1620–21, the people starved. But by the following harvest, God had shown mercy upon them and provided plenty of food. So in thanks, the colonists set aside one day for a bountiful feast. This celebration became Thanksgiving.

A nice story for children, it nevertheless fails in two respects: first, it is not true; second, it doesn't explain the reason for the so-called famine that met them, supposedly only during that first long, hard winter.

What did happen in Plymouth Colony?

Let's run the picture again, this time with the color of human nature intact. There is a spiritual message in the story of Thanksgiving Day. But it is for individuals, not for groups.

There is a spiritual message in the story of Thanksgiving Day. But it is for individuals, not for groups.

243

The scene opens. The *Mayflower*, a ship loaded with Pilgrims from England, stops in the harbor of Plymouth, Massachusetts, and unloads its passengers and their belongings. It is December 1620. Many of the colonists die in that first harsh winter. But spring arrives, and friendly Native Americans teach them how to raise crops in the North American climate. After the harvest that autumn, 1621, the colonists did indeed enjoy a feast of Thanksgiving.

However, there was only enough food for that one community feast. The rest of that second winter in Plymouth Colony saw more famine and death. So the winter of 1621–22 continued to take its toll of colonists' lives.

The next harvest, in 1622, followed the same pattern as the preceding harvest: an autumn feast followed by a third winter of starvation and death.

What was wrong?

William Bradford, the second governor of Plymouth, took a long, hard look at the social organization of the colony. It was basically a socialistic community. The rules of Plymouth Colony, in the words of Governor Bradford, were these: "all profits and benefits that are got by trade, traffic, trucking, working, fishing, or any other means" were to be placed into a common pantry. That was how the colony's larders were to be filled.

How was this store of common goods to be used?

The community law was that "all such persons as are of this colony are to have their meat, drink, apparel, and all provisions out of the common stock." This was socialism.

But the founders of Plymouth Colony had not taken human nature into account when drafting these rules of procedure.

The founders of Plymouth Colony had not taken human nature into account when drafting these rules of procedure.

First, the strong young men of the colony stopped working. They quickly saw that the sweat of their brow was the mainstay of the community, but all they gained from all that labor was an equal share of goods, whose production largely depended upon them. They were the town mules. So they stopped working.

Second, this economic system bred a growing number of parasites: people who could work but refused to, citing illness, age, or gender.

Third, this system led to thievery. At night, neighbors would sneak into the gardens of the more industrious colonists and steal their squash and other vegetables. Soon no one was working. Is it any wonder that the colony experienced famines?

What changes did Governor Bradford make to the economic system?

In 1623, he rewrote the rules. He switched from a society based on community property to one of individual property. He parceled out the land to families. He told them they were responsible for growing their own food and that they could do with the surplus as they pleased. They could eat some, keep a little for the next season's seed, or trade it for money or goods. It was their choice.

So Bradford put an end to socialism at Plymouth Colony.

What happened then? Did the famines of the two previous years continue? Not at all.

As usual, in 1623, the harvest was followed by a day of general Thanksgiving. But unlike the past, the colonists did not starve during the winter that followed, as they had after the crop years of 1621 and 1622. The same pattern of learning about the paralyzing effects of socialism also occurred in other American colonies.

Bradford put an end to socialism at Plymouth Colony. Did the famines of the two previous years continue? Not at all.

Is there a spiritual lesson in this story about the unsuccessful experiment with socialism at Plymouth Colony? Yes, that kind of society is built upon an ignorance of spiritual law.

St. Paul expressed this divine law to early Christians in his second letter to the Thessalonians. In the third chapter he says, "If any would not work, neither should he eat." That's a fairly harsh diet by many of today's standards, but it is an honest one.

The point is not whether socialism is a worse political system than a democracy, for example.

Aristotle, the fourth-century-BC Greek philosopher, had serious doubts about democracy as an ideal state. Perhaps those misgivings had to do with his insight into greed and human nature. When people in a democratic society learn that they can take the property of others by voting for political leaders who gain their power by catering to the greed of the masses, then the spiritual law is put into abeyance.

That spiritual law, by the way, is: Everything must be paid for in the true coin.

That spiritual law, by the way, is: Everything must be paid for in the true coin. That means "if any would not work, neither should he eat." Any time a society puts the rights of its individuals at jeopardy with laws that take away their liberty, property, or free speech without the due process of laws *based on justice*, it is a sign of a spiritually immature society.

This point is not a criticism. It is an observation.

The fact is that earth is an imperfect creation. So no one should look for a perfect society, whether its foundation is one of social or economic or religious values. The question is not whether one society is better than another. Instead, the ECK initiate must ask whether he himself follows the precepts of spiritual law—regardless of the society in which he lives.

There is a very good book about life between lives. It is *Journey of Souls* by Dr. Michael Newton, who holds a doctorate in counseling. In his practice, over ten years, he regressed patients by hypnosis to the interval between one earthly life and their reassignment in the next.

Most of his patients report that no Soul is eternally, irredeemably evil. People make mistakes. Leaders, being human, also make mistakes. There is no guilt fixed upon individuals by teachers, or guides (Lords of Karma), yet nevertheless an erring individual is held fully accountable for the mistakes of his most recent life.

The beliefs of a society—and the people within it—reflect the spiritual development of that society. Some societies are young and immature. Others are more in tune with the spiritual Law of Karma: more mature.

The state of a society is one thing. All societies are a school of sorts where its citizens can learn the spiritual law by trial and error. Our concern is not with any particular form of government.

In ECK, our attention is upon the spiritual unfoldment of each individual. That line of development is unique. Like Soul Itself.

So the key to spiritual freedom, love, and wisdom is the spiritual exercises found in the ECK teachings.

You choose your own direction. You travel at your own pace.

In ECK, our attention is upon the spiritual unfoldment of each individual. That line of development is unique. Like Soul Itself.

45
Like You, All God's Creatures Are Soul Too

A young man from Beijing, China, once wrote to me about the gratitude he felt when a band of ECK missionaries had introduced him to the beautiful love song to God, HU.

But when they left, he felt empty and alone. He wondered why no other people wanted to sing HU with him.

Then, one morning, he heard the beautiful songs of swallows coming from his balcony. It was the first time he'd noticed. He noticed for a reason. He could feel the divine love in their songs, for his great desire for God had opened his spiritual ears. The swallows, he knew, were singing the HU song too.

This brought the realization that he was never alone. God's love was always with him.

Further, the swallows recognized him as a child of God too, so they felt comfortable making a nest on his balcony. When the cold weather came, the swallows flew back to the warm southern part of China.

But he wasn't left alone. Song sparrows moved into the nests, to assure him of God's ever-present love for him.

The swallows, he knew, were singing the HU song too.

"Soul exists because God loves It," says *The Shariyat-Ki-Sugmad*, Book One. And it is truly so. This keystone of ECK is written in the consciousness of all life, and it accounts for some acts of love and charity in the most unusual ways. It showed up in the life of this young Chinese man in the singing of swallows to chase his blues.

But God's love manifests in other ways too.

Wilton, a retired man from Auckland, New Zealand, reported the case of Tiddles, his cat, saving a bird. The story runs like this:

One morning, Wilton heard a loud bang. A blackbird had crashed into a glass panel on his patio. It'd fallen to the seat beneath the window, where it lay stunned. Just that fast, Tiddles was at the scene. Yet she didn't pounce on this blackbird but watched Wilton trying to get it to drink water from a saucer, though without success.

Wilton went inside to get a dropper.

When he returned, an amazing sight greeted his eyes. Tiddles was feeding water to the bird. Her method was inspired.

She'd put her head in the saucer and would lap twice. Then she'd put her dripping mouth to the blackbird's beak, licking it with her tongue. Slowly the bird began to revive. Tiddles watched over it for nearly an hour, at which time it'd gathered its strength and could fly to a low fence. Then it rejoined its mate in a tree, where they'd nested the summer long. It was an amazing sight, indeed.

Dogs, cats, birds, butterflies, guinea pigs, horses, fish, you, and every other living thing are Soul.

Dogs, cats, birds, butterflies, guinea pigs, horses, fish, you, and every other living thing are Soul. There are always a few bright lights among the many dim ones to bring us comfort and joy.

Here is the story of another bright light. This story, too, is about God's love and comfort.

Liz was lonely. She longed for a relationship, but it seemed that life was passing her by. Where was the love and companionship? The blues were her sole companion this Saturday as she returned home from a shopping errand.

She was surprised to see a fluffy white and light orange cat on her door step. It seemed to be waiting for her. The cat let Liz pet him and followed her into the house, inspecting every corner for half an hour. Liz realized the cat was a gift from the ECK, the Holy Spirit. It had come to bring her love. Tears of joy and gratitude blurred her vision.

The two sat on the couch. The cat, on her lap, leaned against her chest and wrapped his big paws almost around her neck. It felt as if he were gently hugging her.

And so the companions sat for the longest time.

After a while, Liz felt lighter and happier and soon was moving about the house, doing chores. The cat had roused too. When Liz returned to the living room, its tail was just disappearing out the front door, which she'd left open for his convenience.

Liz peeked outside an hour later, but the orange and white cat had gone. It had its own home.

Later that same day, another wave of the blues hit her. She sat there, feeling so very alone. Then an image flicked through her mind: The cat was on the door stoop.

Indeed, it was. So they spent the evening together on the couch. She enjoyed TV, while he purred.

Her companion stayed the whole night, stretched out on the comforter under which Liz lay sound asleep. Both she and the cat left her house the next

Liz realized the cat was a gift from the ECK, the Holy Spirit. It had come to bring her love.

Yes, animals are Soul, too, like you.

morning. She was off to the ECK center; he watched her drive away.

He was gone when Liz returned home, and she never saw the beautiful orange and white cat again.

But she knew why he'd come. The ECK had sent him to bring her a gift of divine love, for it can calm a sad and troubled heart.

Yes, animals are Soul, too, like you.

46

When the Right People Do the Right Thing

*S*omeone once said, "Without the Nile there is no Egypt." He was referring to the Nile River overflowing its banks annually, which enriched the soil and made it possible to grow Egypt's grains.

So, too, may we say in Eckankar, "Without the ECK (the Holy Spirit) there is no life."

The ECK is the mainstay of life. Those who obey the spiritual laws of this divine force will naturally do the right thing in the right way. Most people are unconscious agents of this power. They do gain much by it, however, unconscious or not.

A member of Eckankar, though, learns to become more conscious of the ECK and Its ways. To become more aware of the ECK and Its ways requires a new state of consciousness. One who can enter into it sees a broader, richer, and deeper playing out of the workings of creation in the divine order of things. He gets to look behind the scenes. He sees spiritual reasons why certain things are so.

A greater awareness leads to a greater love, both in the seeing and receiving of it.

A member of Eckankar learns to become more conscious of the ECK and Its ways. He gets to look behind the scenes.

Those with a greater state of awareness see more of the reasons behind why things are as they are. So they develop more love and compassion.

These knowers are doers. They help people spiritually by the service they do for them in God's name.

An example of this sort of conscious service is the following experience of a therapist we'll call Claire.

An accomplished pianist once came to Claire for help. This man had a severe block that prevented him from expressing himself in a more fulfilling way, both socially and spiritually. Would Claire try to help him?

Claire took him on as a patient.

Now, she did the right thing in the right way. Claire called upon the Mahanta for help. He is the inner guide for ECKists.

The Mahanta showed Claire one of the pianist's past lives, in which he'd enjoyed wealth and renown. But his personal life was one of debauchery and excess, and that imbalance had come to the foreground in this life. He was now obliged to confront and straighten out the effects of that earlier lifetime.

It was a spiritual necessity. He had to face that hidden side of his history so he could gain in spiritual strength.

There was no easy way out. He had to face himself.

Claire understood what the pianist was up against, that his problem with creating things musically and his weakness in interacting socially with others were of a longstanding nature. There was no quick cure.

Now, she did the right thing in the right way. Claire called upon the Mahanta for help.

But she could help him accommodate to those conditions. Of course, she did not disclose to him the facts of his previous, misspent life. He wouldn't have understood.

So Claire did the right thing in the right way.

Right off, she asked the Mahanta for help. Both she and the pianist benefited from that: she, consciously; he, unconsciously.

In Eckankar, doing the right thing at the right time means to call upon the Mahanta, the Living ECK Master for a second opinion.

Arlene is an ECKist who faced an unpleasant situation. She needed to talk to the principal where her children attended school. It was necessary to explain to him why her children didn't participate in the religious program offered there. She had to tell him about Eckankar.

But Arlene was afraid to do it. She was concerned that her children might suffer harm by the principal learning that they were ECKists.

Yet there was more to it. The principal was an authority figure, and Arlene always had qualms about speaking to those in authority.

For the moment, however, she did nothing.

Then a seemingly unrelated thing happened to her at the hairdresser. Arlene wanted blond highlights in her hair. Part of the hairdresser's procedure was to put a plastic bag over a client's head, covering the forehead and ears.

Arlene's heart began to race.

Then she felt as though she were suffocating, even though her nose and mouth were free.

She felt a deep panic. What on earth was going on? The feeling became so frightening that Arlene was forced to stop the procedure. She apologized to

In Eckankar, doing the right thing at the right time means to call upon the Mahanta, the Living ECK Master for a second opinion.

the hairdresser and returned home.

There, she did the right thing. She put her attention upon the Mahanta. Could he help her?

Immediately, a picture from a past life formed on the inner screen of her mind. Way back, during the medieval Inquisition in Europe, she found herself in a poorly lit cell. There was an iron helmet over her head. It was punishment for her opposing the opinions of church authorities.

The helmet did let her see and breathe; however, she felt trapped. Before long, she went mad.

This past-life experience helped her understand her cowardly attitude in this life when it came to dealing with authorities. A positive result has been this: her greater understanding opened to greater love and spiritual freedom.

Arlene had done the right thing, in the right way.

And such is the challenge and opportunity of living and growing consciously and spiritually. The way, to be sure, lies in the teachings and practices of ECK.

It is so easy to do the right thing when you know how.

Here, then, is a spiritual exercise to help you do that. It's for anytime and anyplace. It can be done even with people around, when circumstances don't allow the opportunity to go off in private.

Put your full, undivided attention upon the face of the Mahanta. Then listen. Wait for some sign or insight for the urgent situation at hand.

Put your full, undivided attention upon the face of the Mahanta. Then listen. Wait for some sign or insight for the urgent situation at hand. It may come as the faintest thought or impression. Again, you may get a very clear, unmistakable picture in your mind's eye of what needs to be done. A past life may come to you subtly.

It is important to trust your inner senses with this spiritual exercise. The Master's advice will be practical and to the point. It will be a sound suggestion. Moreover, it'll feel entirely natural and the right thing to do.

This spiritual exercise does work. However, it requires full confidence in the bond that unites you and the Master.

It is a fulfillment of the Mahanta, the Living ECK Master's ancient promise: "I am always with you."

The Master's advice will be practical and to the point. Moreover, it'll feel entirely natural and the right thing to do.

✳ Spiritual Exercise: A Technique to Go Slower

Life puts you in situations that can cause you to panic. You have to remember to calm down, to get yourself, Soul, back in control of the mind. That helps you think clearly enough to see what needs to be done. Then you can take care of the situation.

Patience and composure are among the attributes of an ECK chela. What can you do to develop these two qualities in yourself?

In contemplation ask the Inner Master what you can do to go slower. Once you've figured out this secret, you can be patient. You can let the storms of life blow over you while you think of a way to find shelter.

One way is through surrender. Tonight, before you go to sleep, speak to the Mahanta. Say, "I am a child of thine. Take me where you will, to show me the ways of Sugmad (God)."

If you slow down, the spiritual principle can begin working through you.

Soul—the spiritual principle, the creative spark of God—cannot work if you panic. Anxiety shuts down the creative centers. When you can't think, whatever you try to do becomes one blunder piled upon another. If you slow down, the spiritual principle can begin working through you so that you can figure out the solution to the problem that is bothering you.

When a student is ready, the Master will appear.

Chapter Nine

A Hunger for God

47
Can Life Be
No More Than This?

an life be no more than this, O Master?"
Such was once a seeker's question to the great ECK Master Rebazar Tarzs (*Stranger by the River*, p. 61). Yes, it can. The weary seeker thirsted mightily for God but didn't know where to look. In time, though, the seeker realized his dream and then became an ECK Master too.

Are the ECK Masters real?

They most certainly are. Read *Those Wonderful ECK Masters*. In this book you'll find many stories by ordinary people who've met them and have thus gained spiritually by it.

For example, a typical story comes from Joan in Vermont. She's been meeting the ECK Masters for a long time now, but lately, she had a special dream with Paul Twitchell that she recalled in a recent letter.

Joan felt she didn't know Paul as well as some of the other ECK Masters. So she decided to approach him.

About three nights later, she had a dream. The first part was like an ECK-Vidya reading of prophecy.

Are the ECK Masters real? Read Those Wonderful ECK Masters. You'll find many stories by ordinary people who've met them and gained spiritually by it.

He was going over her life with her, showing her the areas that called for attention and work. A second part of her dream let her know Paul better.

He took her hands in his and bored into her eyes with those blue eyes of his. Not one word passed between them, yet Joan, in that moment, knew the truth of Paul and his immense love for God and man.

Words were inadequate to tell what she'd learned. But his deep love seared her heart for all time.

She awoke with great joy. She was once again impressed by how asking an ECK Master in sincerity always brings an answer. She also felt a bit foolish. All it took was to ask Paul about Paul.

Life could be no more than this for Joan.

In another instance, ECKists in Rochester, New York, had set up a table at a street festival. A woman approached. She was looking for Soul Travel techniques. She used to leave the body a lot, but now she was on heart medicine and unable to get out of the body at all.

Debby, an ECKist, told her about the HU song and about the protection of a spiritual guide. The woman got short with her right when Debby was handing her a sheet with pictures of the ECK Masters on it.

"I have a guide!" she snapped.

Just when Debby was about to take back the sheet, the woman snatched it back. Her eye had caught something.

"Here he is, that's him!"

She pointed to a picture of Paul Twitchell.

What a wonderful man he was, she said. It's hard to imagine how life could have offered her more than it did at that very moment.

Debby told her about the HU song and about the protection of a spiritual guide.

CAN LIFE BE NO MORE THAN THIS?   265

This last story involves today's Mahanta, the Living ECK Master. His spiritual name is Wah Z.

A man in a light blue denim shirt and blue jeans approached Felix at the trunk of his car. He asked to borrow thirty-five cents. Felix pulled out his wallet and there found only a dollar bill. He turned the wallet upside down and shook it, but it was truly empty.

So Felix handed him the dollar and said, "I'm sorry. I don't have any more."

The stranger replied, "Thanks. I'm glad you didn't judge."

"I do not judge anyone."

"I hope I can do the same for you someday."

"If you don't do it, somebody else will."

Then the stranger walked away, and Felix completely forgot about the incident. But Felix had drawn some books from the library. One was an ECK book, *The Golden Heart*. On the back cover he saw a picture of Wah Z—the stranger!

That night as Felix lay in bed, trying to sort it all out, he heard the same voice of the man he'd spoken to during the day.

It said, "If I did not think you were worthy, I would not have called you."

No, life could be no more than it was at that moment. Felix, like many others over the centuries, thirsted for God yet didn't know where to look. But when a student is ready, the Master will appear.

When a student is ready, the Master will appear.

48
Just Where Does God Fit In?

A member of Eckankar for over twenty-five years has come to a startling realization: he has changed dramatically in his own state of consciousness.

A wonderful gentleman, a member of Eckankar for over twenty-five years, wrote a letter of good spiritual insight to me around the Christmas holiday season.

First, he reflected upon *Stranger by the River*. This book, by Paul Twitchell, is a dialogue between a spiritual seeker and his Master in another time and another place. Twenty-five years ago, this gentleman had dismissed it as being simple and without depth. Yet the book deals with the issues of this world: love, wisdom, life and death, the nature of God and Soul, and others. Those issues are not simple.

Now he has come to a startling realization: he has changed dramatically in his own state of consciousness since then as a member of Eckankar. How did he come to know of the change?

About twenty-five years ago, he gave his first introductory talk on the teachings of ECK. The audience was sizable, about thirty-five people. Like any good convert, this gentleman spoke with conviction about a popular subject then—Soul Travel. He went on and on.

Near the end of his talk, a man at the back of the room raised his hand. "And just where does God fit into all of this?" he asked.

This question set the speaker back on his heels, because he realized he himself had missed the whole point of the ECK teachings. So how could he lecture others?

Soul Travel, dreams, past lives, the ancient science of prophecy, healing, and especially love are all part of the ECK teachings, of course. However, they do not stand alone. They must always be taken in the whole context of Soul's relationship to God. It is this relationship that gives meaning to life. It is the golden tie that binds.

So how did this gentleman learn about his own change of consciousness during the last twenty-five years?

During the most recent Christmas holiday season, he was walking through a shopping mall. The place was full of Christmas decorations. All around him, harried shoppers were flitting from store to store in an attempt to complete their last-minute shopping. Even the piped-in music was urgent. Shop till you drop.

Now he asked himself the same question the man in the back of the lecture room had asked him twenty-five years ago, *And just where does God fit into all of this?*

He reflected upon the chaos around him.

Christmas comes from two words: *Christ* (a state of consciousness) and *mass* (a worship service or celebration). Wasn't Christmas to be a time for Christians to give thanks to God and show gratitude for all the blessings they had received? Wasn't it a season to return a bit of God's love through

He asked himself the same question the man in the lecture room had asked, And just where does God fit into all of this?

offerings of charity and service, to reflect divine love in some way to those around them?

But the shopping mall was a commercial circus.

"What are you going to give me?" and "What am I to get for you?"

This gentleman observed the chaos around him. He had taken a table in the food court of the mall to have a cup of coffee. Half joking, he asked a young man next to him, "I wonder what God would think of all this?"

"What has God to do with it?" replied the young man.

Our friend went home. In his own way, twenty-five years ago he himself had been like that young man. The teachings about Soul Travel, dreams, past lives, the ancient science of prophecy, healing, and especially love are all meaningless unless taken in the context of God's love for Soul. The same holds true for Christmas.

This gentleman reached for *Stranger by the River* and opened it at random. In "The Law of Life" (chapter 31), the ECK Master Rebazar Tarzs reminded him: "When you are full of opinions and speculations, God is withdrawn from thee."

In other words, live and let live.

A dear friend of ours could perhaps ask the question too: "And just where does God fit into all of this?"

He is a successful businessman. Yet lately, a severe drop in the value of his home forced him to sell it at a loss. At the same time a business venture failed. Like so many other successful people, the byways of his life show a lot of losses—certainly not the string of unbroken successes that other people finally view at the end of a long life of ups and downs.

The teachings about Soul Travel, dreams, past lives, the ancient science of prophecy, healing, and especially love are all meaningless unless taken in the context of God's love for Soul.

So currently, our friend has had a few downs in a row. Such an experience is likely to get an individual looking only at past failures, instead of seeing all the areas where his life is blessed: health, a family, love for God and life (despite all recent reverses), and optimism in spite of it all.

His thoughts therefore took a trip down memory lane. Since current losses are so much a part of his life for now, he naturally found his mind searching out earlier losses.

One such experience was a heartbreaker. Especially for a youth.

As a young boy, he had a paper route. To boost subscriptions, the publisher held a contest for the paperboys. The boy who got the most new subscribers to the newspaper in a given period of time would win a trip to Hawaii with his parents.

Our young hero worked hard. So by closing time on the last day of the competition, he had won by turning in thirteen more "starts" than any of the other paperboys. He could just see himself in Hawaii. His proud parents would politely tell any and all who would listen, "Our son won this trip for us by selling newspapers!"

However, there was a small matter of backyard (barnyard?) politics that he hadn't counted on. His chief competitor's father likely had a friend in the publisher's office who passed along the end-of-day totals to him. After all, the expenditure of so much money for three tickets to Hawaii might as well be used to return a favor to a personal friend of someone at the newspaper. Why waste them on just any kid?

Whatever happened is not known.

Somehow, though, his competitor's father learned that our friend was ahead by thirteen starts. So,

Such an experience is likely to get an individual looking only at past failures, instead of seeing all the areas where his life is blessed: health, a family, love for God and life, and optimism in spite of it all.

after hours—after the close of the contest—the father bought twenty newspaper subscriptions for friends and relatives. Then he slipped them through the door of the publisher's office. At night. Someone there approved the illegal subscriptions, and our friend's competitor and his parents got the free trip to Hawaii.

To make matters worse, second prize was a one-speed bike. At a time when three-speed bikes were popular, no self-respecting boy wanted to be seen on a one-speed.

Ashes heaped upon dirt.

A good question for a young boy to ask, "I wonder what God would think of all this?"

Rebazar Tarzs, in *Stranger by the River*, might have answered Soul like this, as he once did the seeker: "Thy experience is nothing less than thy own choices and thoughts made visible" ("The Law of the Self," chapter 12).

Had the boy counted his chicks before they were hatched? Or had his competitor's dishonest father received some sort of tip and special considerations to pay off someone's debt to him?

In the end, does it matter?

Earth is a schoolroom. We're here to have every possible experience. That's how Soul finds spiritual purification and becomes godlike in the end. Why are you here? To make money and get rich? Maybe. There is certainly nothing wrong with money, but what's the use of having it while learning nothing about your spiritual purpose here on earth?

Once more, as Rebazar tells the seeker, "You, yourself, are your own problem. You must understand and act to solve the mystery of thy little self before you can solve the mystery of God."

Earth is a schoolroom. We're here to have every possible experience. That's how Soul finds spiritual purification and becomes godlike in the end.

49
A Seeker Meets
Paul Twitchell

*I*n the introduction to *The Shariyat-Ki-Sugmad*, Book One, Paul Twitchell describes the makeup of these sacred writings of ECK.

"Usually," he says, "it is the spiritual travelers who make it their concern to study this golden book of wisdom and spread its light to those who will listen."

* * *

Paul Twitchell was a spiritual traveler. Later, he became the Mahanta, the Living ECK Master and served as the spiritual head of Eckankar from 1965 to 1971, when he passed over to the inner planes. However, he already knew his coming mission in the 1950s.

The following story is about a young woman who met him then but, true to his prophecy, didn't become a member of Eckankar until many years later. We'll call her May.

May and her husband joined Dianetics groups in the early 1950s. In prior years she'd developed strong psychic abilities, among them the gift of

A young woman met Paul Twitchell in the 1950s but, true to his prophecy, didn't become a member of Eckankar until many years later.

prophecy. Yet she was restless. In fact, they were the indirect cause of her downward spiral from a life of joy to one where all looked flat and shallow.

May and her husband moved from Dallas to Phoenix. There, L. Ron Hubbard had started his fledgling Dianetics organization, which later became the Church of Scientology in 1954. She recalls that Hubbard and Paul Twitchell exchanged information about their spiritual research.

In the midfifties she and her husband attended a packed Scientology convention. May was standing in the hotel lobby with a group, when, one by one, she noticed the group melting away. Even her husband deserted her, telling her to wait there. So she stood alone in the middle of the lobby.

After what felt like ages, he returned. He said someone wished to speak with her and pointed to a small, unimposing man at the fringe of the crowd. He then went back to the wall.

May, stubborn, refused to budge. Finally, her husband returned and gave her a strong push in the stranger's direction. She was furious. Always of an independent and rebellious spirit, she finally relented, determined to get the encounter done with. Later, she saw still pictures and even a movie of him giving a lecture and chastened herself for not seeing his spiritual beauty at the time.

The first thing Paul said was, "You are suffering."

She dismissed her blindness to anger and spiritual immaturity. It was a way to live with herself.

The first thing Paul said was, "You are suffering."

Of course, she was, but May didn't want others to know it. His observation irked her.

"I like to suffer," she snapped.

"You like to suffer?"

"Yes, how else am I going to learn?" In a superior tone, she explained about telling God a long time ago of her willingness to endure the worst hell there was if, in the end, she found what she was searching for.

"Well, you can stop suffering," he said. "You have found me."

What arrogance! she thought.

Despite her psychic powers, she failed to recognize in him the presence of a Master and the future Mahanta. Nor did she realize that her suffering was indeed unnecessary. He could have helped resolve it.

Much of the ensuing conversation was a haze. However, one part about smoking stood out.

Paul told her to stop smoking in front of him. It was the only time he spoke in a stern tone, despite her rudeness. She learned, then and later, of his strong dislike for smoking. In India, May knew, it was a serious breach of etiquette to smoke in the presence of one's guru, father, or older brother.

She refused to honor his request.

Paul persisted, yet he showed grace in spite of her blatant disrespect.

He predicted that she'd follow him when she was sixty; also that she'd speak of this meeting and write about him.

His next words are etched upon her memory:

"You will apologize to me, but it will be too late."

Later, May understood that he'd have passed on; and true to Paul's prediction, she has apologized many times since.

Once more did she see him. It was at a friend's house where Hubbard was also present. Again, May reacted to Paul with hostility, and he left her alone. Never again did she see him in the flesh.

Nor did she realize that her suffering was indeed unnecessary. He could have helped resolve it.

May often cries when she tells this story. She grieves over the poor treatment she dished out to the future Mahanta, and the loss of a golden opportunity to sit at the feet of the Master. But where's the need for shame? There is no need for self-recrimination. The ECK Masters understand. They too once walked in everyman's sandals, turning their backs on the Master due to spiritual immaturity.

The ECK Masters know and understand. They love the seeker in spite of himself. In fact, they love him more than he loves his own defilements.

The next step in spiritual unfoldment is accepting divine love, because it washes away all limitations like guilt and remorse. It must be done. When the individual's consciousness has expanded after enough day-to-day experience, then his Spiritual Eye opens. Pure love and forgiveness will flood his heart. But he must allow it. That's the nature of free will.

May's life took many turns in the years following her meetings with Paul.

One night, a few years later, a Blue Light came and took her out of the body. Only long after did she recognize the source. It was the Blue Light of the Mahanta. Paul was teaching her with the Light and Sound of God, for then followed times of hearing beautiful violin music in the background.

May was a Scientologist through the 1970s. In the 1980s she ran across ads for Eckankar in *Fate* magazine. The HU song in them caught her attention. Then, she also found books on ECK in the library, donated by ECKists. A real blessing.

That's the circuitous route May took to the path of ECK.

One night, a few years later, a Blue Light came and took her out of the body. It was the Blue Light of the Mahanta. Paul was teaching her with the Light and Sound of God.

So long, long ago she'd met Paul in the dawning of his mission. She's come a long way since then.

As *The Shariyat* promises, "The spiritual travelers . . . spread its light to those who will listen." She has.

50
What Is Truth?

 talent scout for a major fashion modeling agency held interviews for young women hoping to crack the ranks of highly paid fashion models. Most failed the interview. The talent scout's dismissal was a curt "Your look is not what we're looking for."

"Well, what are you looking for?" demanded a pretty, young brunette with a petulant toss of her curls.

"I'll know it when I see it," replied the talent scout.

Some consider truth like beauty—a matter of opinion. "Truth is what I make it." These people shop about for it, discover some fad or ideal that meets their comfort level or taste, and embrace it as the absolute truth. Such "truth" includes one's faith in the ideals of their religion or spiritual path as they know them.

An example is two factions of the same religion. One order devotes itself to serving the needs of others, while another tries to gain power and adherents through the abuse of power.

One religion, two quite different approaches to it. Yet both feel that their daily life is to some degree

279

an expression of divine truth.

Jesus and the high priests had different ideas about the nature of truth. The high priests, misusing power, had him arrested and later brought into the judgment hall of Pontius Pilate, the governor. So Pilate asked them, "What's the charge?"

They shuffled their feet, hemmed and hawed, buying time to come up with a little white lie. The best they could do on short notice was a pallid, "Well, if he weren't a criminal, would we have brought him to you?" That put the ball back into Pilate's court.

So Pilate questioned Jesus. In reply to one of Jesus' answers, he said, "What is truth?"

Apparently, he received the only response he was capable of understanding in his state of consciousness—silence. Jesus knew that truth was outside of the governor's pale.

In trying to express truth, many people live a lie.

A while ago a national newspaper ran an article on how wealthy people, and others not so wealthy but well-to-do, wear dirty, faded clothing as a fashion statement. A short time later two readers wrote a response to the editor.

The first letter reflected the stunted self-image of some early Christians. Instead of recognizing how they were made in the image of God and then trying to live up to that, these penitents went about in public like beggars. They wore sackcloth and smeared their bodies with ashes. It was to show how little they thought of their spiritual state.

The author of this letter asked whether today's rich in beggar's clothes were likewise making a public statement about what sorry folks they were inside.

Pilate questioned Jesus, "What is truth?" Jesus knew that truth was outside of the governor's pale.

The second writer made observations just as telling about well-off people in bleached jeans. The fashion cues for the coming season called for clothing embedded with abrasions and grease stains.

Now why wear such rags?

This writer observed it was kids and adults who'd never had to soil their hands as laborers or farmers. But shoddy clothing gave them a false sense of identity.

Talk about self-delusion.

What is truth?

Certainly not a fashion statement that reflects a deceitful image to oneself and others.

What's the main reason that seekers come to the path of ECK?

A recent survey showed most came because their inner senses, intuition, told them the ECK teachings were true. Many found in its teachings the very real fact of personal and spiritual growth. Others, in search of truth, found it through the guidance and love these age-old teachings express.

Many found in the ECK teachings the very real fact of personal and spiritual growth.

Now a question.

How do they know these are the true teachings about life, love, and God? Maybe it's just another state of delusion? Maybe, once again, they're being fooled or are fooling themselves?

Well, maybe. But maybe not. Truth is truth and will stand on its own merit.

The search for truth leads finally to the riddle of God.

ECK Master Rebazar Tarzs, a spiritual traveler of renown, was about to send his student Peddar Zaskq back into the world to practice the Life Force of God within him. This spiritual awareness was newly awakened in the young man.

Yet Zaskq was of a heavy heart. He did not want to leave his friend and teacher to battle the trials of daily living among the masses of Souls out there, blindly stumbling in their search for truth.

Gently, Rebazar told him, "There is no burden that is too great for God. Take whatever It gives with the fullest grace of thy heart, and never feel that ye are without It. God's grace and mercy will pour upon ye, every moment of the day and night. It will watch over thee like the shepherd watches over his flock at all hours."

This "good-bye for now" between teacher and student is reported in "The Riddle of God," *Stranger by the River*, by Paul Twitchell.

Still unconvinced, young Zaskq hesitates to take his leave.

Rebazar, however, has one last thing to impart to him, the riddle of God.

"God is what ye believe It is. No man is wrong about the existence of God, and yet no man is right about his knowledge of God. There is no mystery in God except that It is what each Soul believes that It is. So the riddle is that; but all men will quarrel and argue about the greatness of God and their own knowledge of Him."

Peddar Zaskq looks uncertain.

Rebazar explains.

"Yet every man is right in his knowledge of God. But does this mean that the drunkard is as right as the great minister who preaches from the pulpit? Yea, I say that he, the drunkard, is as much upon the path as the preacher is in his pulpit. . . . Each is in his own place according to his understanding. Ah, but there is the answer."

Yes, there is the answer.

Rebazar explains. "Yet every man is right in his knowledge of God. Each is in his own place according to his understanding."

If one's focus in life is on fads and fashions, his understanding is at the social level instead of the spiritual.

And that's OK. However, there is a greater fullness of truth.

A true seeker has moved beyond the social level and so reaches out to the teachings of ECK. He learns the greater lessons of love and life through his own inner and outer experiences in the Light and Sound of God.

And that is truth.

A true seeker learns the greater lessons of love and life through his own inner and outer experiences in the Light and Sound of God.

51
Personal God
or Supreme God?

There are as many different viewpoints about the Divine Being as there are people. Yet each unique viewpoint about God does share some general characteristics with those of other groups of people.

People and their beliefs about God can be lumped into a few main categories. First, there are those who believe in God. Second, those who don't. Third, those who aren't sure if God exists. Fourth, some who haven't yet arrived at this stage and instead put their attention upon a huge crowd of good and evil spirits. And fifth, there are Souls who don't have the awareness for a concept of God. This group includes the severely retarded and others who for some reason fall outside the main boundaries of a society's religious training.

We're mainly interested in the first three groups.

Of those who believe in God, most believe in a personal God—at least in a Christian society. We'll come back to this category in a minute, because it is the most important one of all for those people who want to advance spiritually.

There are as many different viewpoints about the Divine Being as there are people.

The second group consists of people who don't believe in the existence of God. That's their choice. I have no argument with them or with any of the people who fall into any of the five categories listed above. After all, each person is right about his belief about God, even if that belief refuses to acknowledge any sort of God at all.

It sounds like a paradox, but let me say it again. First, everyone is right in his belief about God. Second, God is so much more than the human mind can encompass that often there is little difference between a believer and an atheist.

A believer may have so many *wrong* notions about God that they outweigh the times he's got it right. So the atheist may stand on even ground. The reason for that is that belief in God must reveal itself in the life of a believer, or it is not a true belief at all. How many times do we see the equivalent of Sunday Christians who act pious one day of the week but spend the other six days cheating, lying, or hurting others?

A true belief about God will reveal itself in someone whom others look up to for love, wisdom, and understanding.

So a true belief about God will reveal itself in an upright individual. He or she is someone whom others look up to for love, wisdom, and understanding.

The third group of people are the agnostics. They honestly don't have any opinion about the existence of God. They do, however, keep the possibility open, especially as they grow older and the end of life draws near. But they may be more spiritual than many people who claim to be believers. Again, a belief in God, a true belief, reveals itself in word and deed. An agnostic may live his life according to the spiritual laws by some deep instinct and so enjoy the love and respect of his family, friends, and acquaintances.

Now the first group bears a closer look. These are the people who profess a belief in God, even though this range may span the far reaches of human consciousness.

Let me say first that God is not a personal God. This means that the Supreme God over all minor gods, however powerful or well-known they may be, does not interfere in the daily lives of people. Instead, there is a spiritual hierarchy to handle the details of every individual's progress, both in this world and those beyond it.

The Supreme God is beyond any conception of the human mind. So any anthropomorphic belief in God is certainly a limited one, although those who believe in such a personal God would be outraged to hear it.

Most people's contact with the divine realm comes through angels, guides, or in the case of ECK members, the Mahanta, the Living ECK Master.

There are two classes of people in this world: those who follow ECK and those who don't. But again, one's spirituality cannot be determined by his membership in one group of believers or another. The spiritual life, you remember, is not one simply of belief. It is one of deeds. How many Christians live up to the principles of their religion? The same question can be asked of ECKists.

Is there a personal God or not? Yes, but he's not the Supreme God.

I've taken a lot of time and effort to help every ECKist learn how to speak about God in their everyday life. So we say God in public instead of Sugmad. Remember that every person's belief about God is unique. We generally patch together some divine qualities that fit into the boundaries of our

The Supreme God is beyond any conception of the human mind.

consciousness, and these qualities become our standards. A higher consciousness will have a broader understanding of God. Moreover, this person will demonstrate the ideals of love, wisdom, understanding, and spiritual freedom in his life.

A highly evolved Soul will be a very responsible person. There won't be much whining about being a victim, having injustices done to him, or never getting the breaks. He knows he is responsible for his own life. If he wants to accomplish a high goal, he is ready to work for it. He doesn't expect someone to give him the rewards of that goal, because spiritual law states that everything must be earned in the true coin.

This person also knows and lives the highest spiritual law: that is, the Law of Love. Do everything with no expectation of reward. It is a hard law to follow, unless one is of a high state of consciousness. Then it comes naturally.

One who is a strong believer in a personal God often does not know about the Law of Cause and Effect. Or he may not know the Law of Love. A highly evolved spiritual being knows both and lives them.

A highly evolved Soul pulls his own irons out of the fire.

There also lies the difference between a belief in a personal God and a God who is simply love but has made arrangements for the smallest needs of every creature. These arrangements by the Supreme God are carried out through a very elaborate spiritual hierarchy. People who are in an adolescent stage of unfoldment often make contact with angels, teachers, or guides and mistake them for God—a personal God. It's a play of illusion upon the human ego.

A highly evolved Soul pulls his own irons out of

the fire. Knowing the Law of Cause and Effect, he knows he put them there in the first place. A less evolved Soul doesn't understand the Law of Compensation: "Whatsoever a man sows, that also shall he reap." So he expects a personal God to pull his irons from the fire. *Deus ex machina*—the god of the ancient Greek plays.

We all like to think that whatever we believe or belong to is of the very highest nature. Often, it's not. But don't try to tell anyone else that his God is simply a minor god. Even if it's true. People do not like to hear the truth if it goes against their pet beliefs.

Personal God or Supreme God? It's certainly not an issue to fight over, because that would prove that one's belief about God is an immature one.

Let people be. Don't get drawn into an argument about whether your God is more divine than the God of someone else. As a true Co-worker with the Mahanta, in fact, you would probably support the honest beliefs of others, as long as they uplift and build people and don't tear anyone down.

In Eckankar, our aspirations are set toward becoming a Co-worker with God. That means to love and serve our fellow beings because of our unswerving love for Sugmad, the Supreme God of all.

In Eckankar, our aspirations are set toward becoming a Co-worker with God. That means to love and serve our fellow beings because of our unswerving love for God.

52
A Hunger for God

An old saying has it that "whose bread I eat, his song I sing."

This proverb, in use before the twelfth century, described a common situation in the Middle Ages. Namely, that an itinerant musician who stopped a few days at a noble's castle would be asked to sing and play for the noble's guests. In exchange, the troubadour received gifts of coin and lodging.

So it was understood he'd perform music to suit the noble's taste.

The saying was a colorful way to explain the loyalty and service due a benefactor. It encompassed both traveling musicians and also the serfs of a kind and generous lord.

In spiritual terms, the proverb boils down to loyalty from gratitude.

A hunger for God is but the germ of a passion at the outset of an individual's excursion into the land of karma and reincarnation. It develops over the ages. Hardship, pain, toil, misery, loneliness, and disappointment are its culture. So this hunger for God grows and grows.

A hunger for God is but the germ of a passion at the outset of an individual's excursion into the land of karma and reincarnation. It develops over the ages.

Lifetime upon lifetime of misadventure later, this battered wanderer comes upon good fortune. He happens upon the teachings of ECK.

Now the real tests begin.

A pure spiritual enlightenment outshines the simple mental admonition of *gnothi seauton*, an ancient Greek philosopher's appeal: "know thyself." A spiritual one gives more than the dim flickering of a candle to examine the workings of one's whole being. It is a white-hot fire. This divine flame sears the heart, mind, and being—leaving behind a pure heart and consciousness. It scorches away the most base properties within a seeker, making of him a fit and pure utensil or vessel to handle or contain the meat and drink at the table of the Most High.

In due season this wanderer finds the teachings of ECK. He's come home, to the land of impossible dreams.

In due season this wanderer finds the teachings of ECK.

He's come home, to the land of impossible dreams. A place of love, shelter, freedom and, yes, freely given service.

How does the final chapter in a wanderer's sojourn play out in real time? How will he know truth? Will he stumble upon it? Or, does it require the final scaling of a mighty cliff to reach it?

Who can say?

All come to Eckankar by unique paths. Some wade through marshes, some thread an uncertain path out of a dark and foreboding forest, others brave an unforgiving desert, while a fortunate few find an easy passage through birth into an ECK family.

But all have one thing in common: a hunger for God.

So let's look a minute at the case of Chris. One day he called the Eckankar Spiritual Center to start his membership. Over the years, he said, he'd come across the ECK teachings from time to time. But the hunger wasn't urgent yet.

Then, a few days earlier, he went on, he saw an ECK ad in a local Oregon paper.

A strong nudge said, "Call the ECK center." There is one in his town, but his calls didn't go through. So he turned to the Internet. The Eckankar site suggested he call Membership Services in Minneapolis to help with his situation. Yet the office was closed. In desperation from the spiritual hunger that ravaged his heart, he begged the Mahanta, the Living ECK Master for help that night.

The very next day his computer went on the blink. He called a technician to fix it.

Chris and the technician alike saw a familiarity in each other's face. Years ago, it turned out, both had belonged to the same support group. A small world.

Then, out of the blue, the tech rep asked Chris if he'd ever heard of Eckankar.

"Heard of it?" Chris said. "I've been trying to get in touch with it."

Their chance meeting turned into a discussion about the teachings of ECK. Right after that, Chris called the ECK Spiritual Center in Minneapolis to request a membership. His excitement was such that he couldn't get off the phone. He wondered why he'd waited so long. Everything he'd heard and read on the Internet about ECK fell in line with already held beliefs.

Gratitude and joy filled Chris. In a real sense, he was a wandering Soul who'd come home.

Of course, the tests go on. Layer upon layer of delusion are peeled away like onion skin until only

Out of the blue, the tech rep asked Chris if he'd ever heard of Eckankar. "Heard of it?" Chris said. "I've been trying to get in touch with it."

Soul, the True Self, remains. Facing oneself does take courage. The webs, dust, and clutter of an impure state of consciousness can be troubling. But divine grace, love, and gratitude accomplish a full housecleaning, top to bottom.

What does this purification offer?

There's another saying: "If you like who, what, and where you are, you will be happy." The ECK (Holy Spirit) goes beyond *gnothi seauton*, for It reaches into one's innermost being, far beyond the play of the mind. It brings you into accord with God's love.

There are lots of stories about the ways members of Eckankar have found ECK and of the many occasions the Mahanta, the Inner Master, has helped them with healing, protection, or an outpouring of divine love. I write not to bend anyone's arm. I make no attempt to convert any heart. The Masters of ECK know and teach that when an individual has a real hunger for God, he will seek out the Lord's table on his own. Only then will they aid his quest.

And so it truly is.

It is for that very reason that I try to tell it like it is. One is either ready or he is not. In the end, persuasion used in some religions to get converts leads to grief all around. A hunger for God will eventually turn an individual to searching again until he finds ECK.

So with love and goodwill, I welcome you to the family of ECK. Dine now at the high table. Here, your driving hunger may find peace and satisfaction.

With love and goodwill, I welcome you to the family of ECK. Here, your driving hunger may find peace and satisfaction.

✴ Spiritual Exercise: The Temple Door

This is a very simple exercise to make contact with the Voice of God.

Close your eyes and relax. You are preparing to enter the inner temple, that sacred place where Soul has communication with God. You may see the Light of God first in your Spiritual Eye. You may see It as a Blue Light or a Blue Star. You may see It as a globe or blob of light.

This means you have contact with the highest state of consciousness that is available. It can uplift you to that very same state, too, but not overnight—the shock would be too great.

After you see the Light in your Spiritual Eye or feel It in your heart center, then comes the Sound. The Sound may come first at times.

The Sound may be that of the flute of God which comes from the Soul Plane. Or you may hear the buzzing of bees or any number of different sounds. Later, as you move higher, it may become a very high peeping sound, a single peep so high that it feels as if you can barely reach it.

It is the Voice of God uplifting you.

You are preparing to enter the inner temple, that sacred place where Soul has communication with God.

GLOSSARY

Words set in SMALL CAPS are defined elsewhere in this glossary.

ARAHATA. *ah-rah-HAH-tah* An experienced and qualified teacher of ECKANKAR classes.

BLUE LIGHT. How the MAHANTA often appears in the inner worlds to the CHELA or seeker.

CHELA. *CHEE-lah* A spiritual student. Often refers to a member of ECKANKAR.

ECK. *EHK* The Life Force, the Holy Spirit, or Audible Life Current which sustains all life.

ECKANKAR. *EHK-ahn-kahr* Religion of the Light and Sound of God. Also known as the Ancient Science of SOUL TRAVEL. A truly spiritual religion for the individual in modern times. The teachings provide a framework for anyone to explore their own spiritual experiences. Established by PAUL TWITCHELL, the modern-day founder, in 1965. The word means "Co-worker with God."

ECK MASTER(S). Spiritual Masters who can assist and protect people in their spiritual studies and travels. The ECK Masters are from a long line of God-Realized SOULS who know the responsibility that goes with spiritual freedom.

FUBBI QUANTZ. *FOO-bee KWAHNTS* The guardian of the SHARIYAT-KI-SUGMAD at the Katsupari Monastery in northern Tibet. He was the MAHANTA, the LIVING ECK MASTER during the time of Buddha, about 500 BC.

GOD-REALIZATION. The state of God Consciousness. Complete and conscious awareness of God.

HU. *HYOO* The most ancient, secret name for God. The singing of the word *HU* is considered a love song to God. It can be sung aloud or silently to oneself.

INITIATION. Earned by a member of ECKANKAR through spiritual unfoldment and service to God. The initiation is a private ceremony in which
the individual is linked to the Sound and Light of God.

KAL NIRANJAN, THE. *KAL nee-RAHN-jahn* The Kal; the negative power,
also known as Satan or the devil.

KARMA, LAW OF. The Law of Cause and Effect, action and reaction, justice,
retribution, and reward, which applies to the lower or psychic worlds:
the Physical, Astral, Causal, Mental, and Etheric planes.

KLEMP, HAROLD. The present MAHANTA, the LIVING ECK MASTER. Sri Harold
Klemp became the Mahanta, the Living ECK Master in 1981. His
spiritual name is WAH Z.

LIVING ECK MASTER. The title of the spiritual leader of ECKANKAR. His duty
is to lead SOUL back to God. The Living ECK Master can assist
spiritual students physically as the Outer Master, in the dream state
as the Dream Master, and in the spiritual worlds as the Inner Master.

MAHANTA. *mah-HAHN-tah* A title to describe the highest state of God
Consciousness on earth, often embodied in the LIVING ECK MASTER.
He is the Living Word. An expression of the Spirit of God that is
always with you. Sometimes seen as a Blue Light or Blue Star or in
the form of the Mahanta, the Living ECK Master.

MAHDIS. *MAH-dees* The initiate of the Fifth Circle (SOUL PLANE); often
used as a generic term for all High Initiates in ECK.

PEDDAR ZASKQ. *PEH-dahr ZASK* The spiritual name for PAUL TWITCHELL,
the modern-day founder of ECKANKAR and the MAHANTA, the
LIVING ECK MASTER from 1965 to 1971.

PLANE(S). The levels of existence, such as the Physical, Astral, Causal,
Mental, Etheric, and SOUL planes.

REBAZAR TARZS. *REE-bah-zahr TAHRZ* A Tibetan ECK MASTER known as
the torchbearer of ECKANKAR in the lower worlds.

SELF-REALIZATION. SOUL recognition. The entering of Soul into the Soul
PLANE and there beholding Itself as pure Spirit. A state of seeing,
knowing, and being.

SHAMUS-I-TABRIZ. *SHAH-muhs-ee-tah-BREEZ* Guardian of the SHARIYAT-
KI-SUGMAD on the Causal PLANE. He was the MAHANTA, the LIVING ECK
MASTER in Ancient Persia.

SHARIYAT-KI-SUGMAD. *SHAH-ree-aht-kee-SOOG-mahd* The sacred scriptures of ECKANKAR. The scriptures are comprised of about twelve
volumes in the spiritual worlds. The first two were transcribed from
the inner PLANES by PAUL TWITCHELL, modern-day founder of ECKANKAR.

SOUL. The True Self. The inner, most sacred part of each person. Soul
exists before birth and lives on after the death of the physical body.

As a spark of God, Soul can see, know, and perceive all things. It is the creative center of Its own world.

SOUL TRAVEL. The expansion of consciousness. The ability of SOUL to transcend the physical body and travel into the spiritual worlds of God. Soul Travel is taught only by the LIVING ECK MASTER. It helps people unfold spiritually and can provide proof of the existence of God and life after death.

SOUND AND LIGHT OF ECK. The Holy Spirit. The two aspects through which God appears in the lower worlds. People can experience them by looking and listening within themselves and through SOUL TRAVEL.

SPIRITUAL EXERCISES OF ECK. The daily practice of certain techniques to get us in touch with the Light and Sound of God.

SRI. *SREE* A title of spiritual respect, similar to reverend or pastor, used for those who have attained the Kingdom of God. In ECKANKAR, it is reserved for the MAHANTA, the LIVING ECK MASTER.

SUGMAD. *SOOG-mahd* A sacred name for God. SUGMAD is neither masculine nor feminine; It is the source of all life.

TEMPLE(S) OF GOLDEN WISDOM. These Golden Wisdom Temples are spiritual temples which exist on the various PLANES—from the Physical to the Anami Lok; CHELAS of ECKANKAR are taken to the temples in the SOUL body to be educated in the divine knowledge; the different sections of the SHARIYAT-KI-SUGMAD, the sacred teachings of ECK, are kept at these temples.

TWITCHELL, PAUL. An American ECK MASTER who brought the modern teachings of ECKANKAR to the world through his writings and lectures. His spiritual name is Peddar Zaskq.

VAHANA. *vah-HAH-nah* Vehicle; carrier of ECK or the message of ECK; the ECK missionary.

VAIRAG. *vie-RAHG* Detachment.

WAH Z. *WAH zee* The spiritual name of SRI HAROLD KLEMP. It means the Secret Doctrine. It is his name in the spiritual worlds.

For more explanations of ECKANKAR terms, see *A Cosmic Sea of Words: The ECKANKAR Lexicon* by Harold Klemp.

BIBLIOGRAPHY

"Another Look at *The Shariyat*." *The Mystic World*, June 2002.

"The Art of Soul Travel." *The Mystic World*, December 1996.

"Behind the Scenes with Paul Twitchell." *The Mystic World*, March 2003.

"The Breadth and Depth of the ECK Initiation." *The Mystic World*, March 2002.

"Can Life Be No More Than This?" *The Mystic World*, March 2006.

"Change Is, Oh, So Hard." *The Mystic World*, December 2002.

"The Dark Night of Soul." *The Mystic World*, December 2003.

"The Fantastic Spiritual Quest of Milarepa." *The Mystic World*, June 2005.

"From Ashes to Cathedral." *The Mystic World*, June 2001.

"From the Master's Chair." *The Mystic World*, June 2004.

"Game of Chess." Klemp, Harold. *The Spiritual Exercises of ECK* (ECKANKAR: Minneapolis, 1993, 1997).

"God Loves Pets Too." *Eckankar Journal*, 1998.

"God's River of Love." *ECK Spirituality Today*, 2002.

"God Waits for You within the Problem." *The Mystic World*, December 1998.

"Grow or Go." *The Mystic World*, September 2000.

"Heaven's Narrow Door." *The Mystic World*, December 1999.

"How to Find Freedom from Yourself." *The Mystic World*, September 1998.

"How to Find Spiritual Freedom in This Lifetime." *Eckankar Journal*, 1999.

"A Hunger for God." *Eckankar Journal*, 2004.

"In God's Time and in God's Way." *The Mystic World*, March 2005.

"Just Where Does God Fit In?" *Eckankar Journal*, 1997.

"Like You, All God's Creatures Are Soul Too." *Eckankar Journal*, 2006.

"The Lion and the Ass." *The Mystic World*, December 2000.

"Mahanta, I Love You." *The Spiritual Exercises of ECK*.

"The Master's Presence." *The Spiritual Exercises of ECK*.

"The Mountain of God." *The Spiritual Exercises of ECK*.

"The Nightingale's Song." *The Mystic World*, September 2003.

"Oh, You've Come So Far!" *The Mystic World*, September 2006.

"One Small Change." *The Mystic World*, June 1999.

"On the Rooftops." *The Spiritual Exercises of ECK*.

"The Open Heart." *The Spiritual Exercises of ECK*.

"Our Greatest Teachers." *The Mystic World*, March 2004.

"Past, Present, and Future Lives." *Eckankar Journal*, 2003.

"Paul Twitchell in Context of the Times." *The Mystic World*, June 2003.

"Personal God or Supreme God?" *The Mystic World*, September 1996.

"Purification by Initiation." *The Mystic World*, December 2004.

"Renovations of the Heart." *The Mystic World*, September 1999.

"A Seeker Meets Paul Twitchell." *The Mystic World*, September 2002.

"Sharing What You Love." *The Mystic World*, September 2005.

"A Single Yellow Rose." *The Mystic World*, June 2000.

"Soul Travel and the Continuity of Life." *The Mystic World*, December 2005.

"The Spiritual Lie of Socialism." *The Mystic World*, June 1996.

"The Spiritually Great." *The Mystic World*, December 2001.

"The Spiritual Years of ECK." *The Mystic World*, March 1997.

"A Technique to Go Slower." *The Spiritual Exercises of ECK*.

"The Temple Door." *The Spiritual Exercises of ECK*.

"A Test in a Dream Doctor's Office." *The Mystic World*, September 1997.

"Two-part Door of Soul." Klemp, Harold. *Past Lives, Dreams, and Soul Travel* (ECKANKAR: Minneapolis, 2003).

"Wanna-be Prophets, Dream Analysts, and Other Guides." *The Mystic World*, March 1998.

"What Is Truth?" *ECK Spirituality Today*, 2001.

"When One Door Closes . . ." *The Mystic World*, March 2001.

"When the Right People Do the Right Thing." *Eckankar Journal*, 2005.

"When Worlds Collide or Burn." *The Mystic World*, September 2001.

"Who You Are Speaks Loudly." *The Mystic World*, March 2000.

"Why People Don't Find Spiritual Freedom." *The Mystic World*, June 1998.

"Will Your Love Grow?" *The Mystic World*, December 1997.

"The Wonder of You." *The Mystic World*, September 2004.

"Yes, Aesop's Animal Stories Still Speak to Us Today." *Eckankar Journal*, 2000.

"You, the Master, and Change." *The Mystic World*, June 1997.

"Your Key to the Secret Worlds." *The Mystic World*, March 1996.

"Your State of Consciousness Is Your State of Acceptance." *The Mystic World*, March 1999.

INDEX

wannabes, 81–82
war(s), 231–32. *See also* First
    Crusade
Washington, George, 20, 103
water riddle, 95–96
Way of the Eternal, 38, 136, 213.
will, 194
Winfrey, Oprah, 181, 184
wisdom, 20, 27, 35, 213, 267
  book of, 273
  to do nothing, 63
  of the ECK, 141
  recognizing the gift of this life,
    226
  Soul grows in, 101
  use love and, to make this a
    better place, 232
wolf fable, 50–51
word(s)
  holy, 136 (*see also* HU)
  initiate's personal, 104, 105,

119, 144
Word of God, 138, 198. *See also*
    ECK; Holy Spirit; Light and
    Sound of God; Voice of God
workshop(s), 183, 184
world(s)
  of ECK, 204
  of God, 44, 76, 209
  inner, 109, 172
  key to secret, 44, 46
  of matter, 141–42
  outer, 172
  parallel, 109
  we make our own, 8
World Trade Center, 131
worthiness, 14

Years of ECK, Spiritual. *See*
    Spiritual Years of ECK

321

FOR FURTHER READING AND STUDY

Those Wonderful ECK Masters
Harold Klemp

Could you be one of the countless people who have been touched by a meeting with an ECK Master? These real-life stories and spiritual exercises can awaken you to the presence and help of these spiritual guides. Since the beginning of time they have offered guidance, protection, and divine love to help you fulfill your spiritual destiny.

Past Lives, Dreams, and Soul Travel
Harold Klemp

What if you could recall past-life lessons for your benefit today? What if you could learn the secret knowledge of dreams to gain the wisdom of the heart? Or Soul Travel, to master the shift in consciousness needed to find peace and contentment? To ride the waves of God's love and mercy? Let Harold Klemp, leading authority in all three fields, show you how.

How to Survive Spiritually in Our Times,
Mahanta Transcripts, Book 16
Harold Klemp

A master storyteller, Harold Klemp weaves stories, tips, and techniques into the golden fabric of his talks. They highlight the deeper truths within you, so you can apply them in your life *now*. He speaks right to Soul. It is that divine, eternal spark that you are. The survivor. Yet survival is only the starting point in your spiritual life. Harold Klemp also shows you how to gain in spiritual wealth. This book's a treasure.

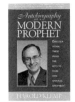

Autobiography of a Modern Prophet
Harold Klemp

Master your true destiny. Learn how this man's journey to God illuminates the way for you too. Dare to explore the outer limits of the last great frontier, your spiritual worlds! The more you explore them, the sooner you come to discovering your true nature as an infinite, eternal spark of God. This book helps you get there! A good read.

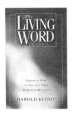

The Living Word, Book 2
Harold Klemp

This collection of articles by Harold Klemp from 1989 to 1995 will help you become stronger, more self-reliant, and capable of discovering spiritual truths in your daily life. If you uncover only a tenth of the spiritual truth and divine love within its pages, you'll be transformed into a nobler state of being many times over.

The Shariyat-Ki-Sugmad, Books 1 and 2

The "Way of the Eternal." These writings are the scriptures of ECKANKAR. They speak to you directly and come alive in your heart.

Stranger by the River
Paul Twitchell

A poetic dialogue between the ECK Master Rebazar Tarzs and the Seeker. Through their conversation, you'll discover the nature of God, love, wisdom, freedom, purity, and death. Its classic style is reminiscent of Kahil Gibran's *The Prophet*.

The Tiger's Fang
Paul Twitchell

Paul Twitchell's teacher, Rebazar Tarzs, takes him on a journey through vast worlds of Light and Sound, to sit at the feet of the spiritual Masters. Their dialogue brings out the secret of how to draw closer to God—and awaken Soul to Its spiritual destiny.

Available at bookstores, online booksellers, or directly from Eckankar: www.Eckankar.org; (952) 380-2222; ECKANKAR, Dept. BK66, PO Box 2000, Chanhassen, MN 55317-2000 USA.

There May Be an Eckankar Study Group near You

Eckankar offers a variety of local and international activities for the spiritual seeker. With hundreds of study groups worldwide, Eckankar is near you! Many areas have Eckankar centers where you can browse through the books in a quiet, unpressured environment, talk with others who share an interest in this ancient teaching, and attend beginning discussion classes on how to gain the attributes of Soul: wisdom, power, love, and freedom.

Around the world, Eckankar study groups offer special one-day or weekend seminars on the basic teachings of Eckankar. For membership information, visit the Eckankar Web site (**www.Eckankar.org**). For the location of the Eckankar center or study group nearest you, click on "Eckankar around the World" for a listing of those areas with Web sites. You're also welcome to check your phone book under **ECKANKAR**; call **(952) 380-2222, Ext. BK66**; or write **ECKANKAR, Att: Information, BK66, PO Box 2000, Chanhassen, MN 55317-2000 USA.**

☐ Please send me information on the nearest Eckankar center or study group in my area.

☐ Please send me more information about membership in Eckankar, which includes a twelve-month spiritual study.

Please type or print clearly

Name _____
first (given)   last (family)

Street _____ Apt. # _____

City _____ State/Prov. _____

Zip/Postal Code _____ Country _____

ABOUT THE AUTHOR

Harold Klemp was born in Wisconsin and grew up on a small farm. He attended a two-room country schoolhouse before going to high school at a religious boarding school in Milwaukee, Wisconsin.

After preministerial college in Milwaukee and Fort Wayne, Indiana, he enlisted in the U.S. Air Force. There he trained as a language specialist at Indiana University and a radio intercept operator at Goodfellow AFB, Texas. Then followed a two-year stint in Japan where he first encountered Eckankar.

In October 1981, he became the spiritual leader of Eckankar, Religion of the Light and Sound of God. His full title is Sri Harold Klemp, the Mahanta, the Living ECK Master. As the Living ECK Master, Harold Klemp is responsible for the continued evolution of the Eckankar teachings.

His mission is to help people find their way back to God in this life. Harold Klemp travels to ECK seminars in North America, Europe, and the South Pacific. He has also visited Africa and many countries throughout the world, meeting with spiritual seekers and giving inspirational talks. There are many videocassettes and audiocassettes of his public talks available.

325

326

In his talks and writings, Harold Klemp's sense of humor and practical approach to spirituality have helped many people around the world find truth in their lives and greater inner freedom, wisdom, and love.

International Who's Who of Intellectuals
Ninth Edition

Reprinted with permission of Melrose Press Ltd., Cambridge, England, excerpted from *International Who's Who of Intellectuals, Ninth Edition*, Copyright 1992 by Melrose Press Ltd.